DARE TO BE

Limitless!

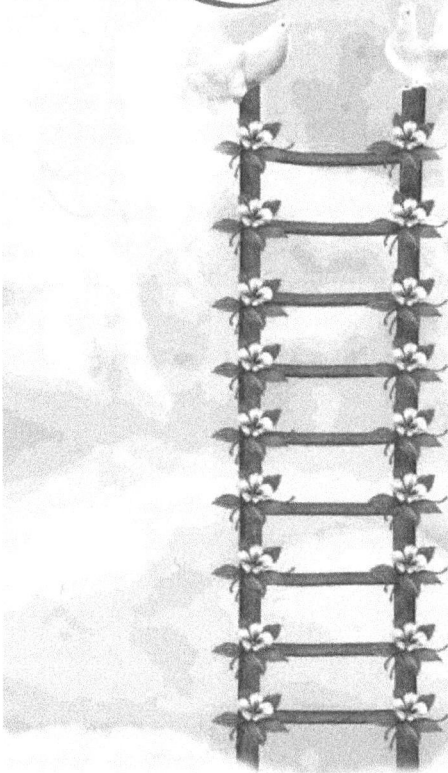

When the Angels Take Your Hand

ELSA J. STOKES, PH.D.

Dare to be Limitless! (When the Angels take Your Hand)
Copyright © 2011 by Elsa J. Stokes, Ph.D.

ISBN 9780615497211

Printed by Dream Hawk Media.
(www.dreamhawkmedia.com)

Book Designer, Illumination Graphics, Deborah Perdue.

To my Angels--my Loving Husband Carey, my Angelic Mom Luz, my Almost Twin Sister Angela, my Adorable Stepson Dillon, my Talented Father Jaime, and my Heartfelt Brother Mario, I give you thanks for inspiring me and shining your light so brightly on me.

Acknowledgments

This book would not have been possible without the inspiration and guided help of my trusted Angels. They showed me the way and have their hands in every single chapter. I want to thank my wonderful husband Carey Stokes for encouraging me and standing by my side, for never giving up on me, for sacrificing his time and his energy in helping me, and for sacrificing our time together to make sure I would be available to write this book.

My gratitude goes out to Lora A. Tucker for having the hardest job of all; understanding my handwriting and typing the words in record speed to complete this book. My heart is with Linda Jay Geldens, Copyeditor/Copywriter. She is a very talented Angel whom God sent me to edit this book. *She helped communicate the Angels' messages with style*

I would also like to thank my fabulous sister Angela Curci, for always being there for me, every time I needed her. She is always by my side, no matter where I go.

I would like to thank my sweet Stepson Dillon Stokes who has always been such an inspiration to me.

I would also like to thank my wonderful sister Irene Ramirez for always supporting me.

And lastly, I would like to thank my incredible Mom, Luz Ramirez, for always believing in me since the day I was born, for being an example of pure love in my life and what it is like to be made of love and only love.

Table of Contents

Foreword

Elsa Stokes was born a natural Medium; she is extremely psychic, and has always been connected to her Angels.

Since birth she has been blessed by God with the gift of prophecy. Knowing what would happen next always gave her a sense of comfort, but nothing could prepare her for her near- death experience, when the Angels took her hand and gave her the choice to come back. Before her return, the Angels empowered her to live a limitless life.

Today God still shows Elsa her every tomorrow, yet she knows that her thoughts, her words, her choices and her determination are really what make the movie in her head play today what will happen tomorrow.

Experience the Angels taking your hand and guiding you to break through the barriers of your perceived limitations. With the various proven methods and techniques found in this book, you can experience limitless possibilities.

The universe is rich with an unlimited supply of all that you desire; it is alive with many new dimensions and levels.

Dare to be limitless, discover your original destiny, and step into your true divinity.

Preface

I would like to start this book with a prayer that everyone who reads this book receives a healing, rather it be miraculous or any other type. May this book help you heighten your intuition to the highest degree. Whatever we concentrate on expands. I believe books can help us make everlasting changes. I have read books that have helped me evolve, grow, seek and continue seeking. Know that we are constantly growing; we never stay the same.

The Angels guided me to write this book, gave me the title and the content. I hope that my experience will empower you to make small or big steps to remove all sorts of limitations that may be holding you back from your true destiny, your God- given divinity.

I do not pretend to know everything, and nor do I believe I have all the answers. What I do know is that the Angels gave me their messages to share with you, to take to heart the power of Spirit, and all that the Angels and Spirit can do for you. Enjoy.

Introduction

I have written this book because the Angels have been telling me that it was time I get these messages out to you.

Angels are celestial beings who have no judgment and are here to assist us in every area of our life. They want to make it clear to us that we do not have any limitations in life, and that all things are possible.

There are certain techniques and exercises we can do to change our outcome in life, to manifest what we truly desire.

We are magnetic beings; we simply have to recognize our power and put that power into action.

In this book you will read stories about circumstances that you might find hard to believe, but hold on to your hat, because some of the stories might shock you. This is a nondenominational book, with guided meditations and exercises that will help rid you of any limitations.

You will hear first from the departed and get clear messages of what they are capable of doing.

You will see that there are no coincidences in life and that much of our life has already been written. However, you will also find that our thoughts today determine our tomorrows.

This is a spiritual book with spiritual content.
You will travel with me when I experience my near-death experience, and you will get a taste of what it feels like to be in the presence of an Angel.

Our greatest glory is in never falling, but in getting up every time we do. (Confucius)

Go confidently in the direction of your dreams. Live the life you have imagined. (Henry David Thoreau)

Chapter One
The Family

Born into a family of twelve, I never really felt alone. With nine girls and three boys roaming around the house, I was always surrounded by family or someone close to me. Yet oftentimes I found myself wanting to be alone. I wanted to play with my Dear Angels, Spirit Guides and deceased Loved Ones. At the time I could tell that these guides, these celestial beings, were different from my brothers, my sisters and anyone I knew. I loved this about the Angels. No one else could see them but me, and I was OK with that. I did not care what anyone else thought. I only knew what I saw.

Growing up seeing everything before it happened was also quite a challenge because it was just a fact. I had to deal with a lot of guilt, especially if I did not get a chance to tell someone what was going to happen before it did. I thought that perhaps if I told, then it would not happen. What I discovered was that oftentimes, even when I told someone what I saw was going to happen, he or she did not listen. And then it would happen anyway. I wondered why God was letting me know what the future was, if I could not do anything about it.

I also never understood why I could "remote-view." I could see things that were going on in different places in the world, what people were doing, what they were talking about, even what they were wearing. It was like watching many movies all at the same time, a few seconds apart.

God would show me the exact words someone was going to say and play the entire scene in my head before it would happen. For example, one day I told my sister Angela to go to the nearby 7-11 convenience store to prove to her that I could predict what would happen. I told her, "At the 7-11, you will see a man wearing a striped yellow-and-orange shirt. He is tall, dark-haired, standing in the back of the store. He will tell you these exact words; "Hi, how are you? You have beautiful hair. It must take you a long time to wash, since it is so thick?" You will laugh and say, "No, not so bad." You will then buy an ice cream cone and come back home." She was so impressed, and was eager to see if what I was telling her was true.

She came back laughing her head off because this actually happened, and she was so fascinated by this game that she wanted to continue playing. I asked her if she thought this happens to other people, and she said, "Of course not." At that point I knew I should not express my psychic gifts to anyone because they would think I was weird.

I remember an accident that happened in my family. It left me feeling very bad. Although I expressed my concerns to my sisters, no one wanted to listen. I had a vision the night before that something terrible would happen to one of my sisters. The next day, as two of my sisters were crossing the street, my sister Irene got run over by a drunk driver who was going 60 miles an hour. He had not seen her.

The next day, I was home, my Mom picked up the phone and another sister said, sobbing, "Irene is dead. She got run over by a car." That sister could not believe that anyone could survive such an accident. I told my Mom, "No, Irene is not dead" because since I had seen it in my vision, I knew how it would all pan out. The paramedics could not believe that she survived, since her body flew two blocks away. But everything I saw in the vision is exactly how it happened. When you receive a vision it is just like a movie, with absolutely no changes.

What happened was that my sister Irene was not able to walk normally and move on with her life until five years after the accident happened. I did not feel guilty about this incident because I had let everyone know what would happen the night before. But I felt really bad that I could not stop it. I remember practically getting on my knees begging my sisters not to go out.

My Dad had a similar gift. He was able to tap into his past lives without having to go into a past life regression meditation. He told me that God had given me many gifts and that I was supposed to use them to help others. I have been very fortunate to have had a Dad and a Mom who support me.

I can only imagine going through this experience without my parents by my side, understanding me and telling me I would be OK. They told me that it was all God's plan for me, to open up to the good aspects of the gift that being a prophet holds and not look at the negative aspect. I always thought perhaps I would end up on TV one day, interviewed as a freak because I can see the future. So I kept my gift a secret for a very long time.

During this time in my life, there were no Mediums doing readings, or any metaphysical activities going on. It was all about Jesus or whatever has to do with organized religion.

Chapter Two
Touched by an Angel

I never really knew my Grandmother Alicia. We came to the United States when I was only two years old. I do not recall hearing much about her while we were growing up either. As I said earlier, I was born with the gift of prophecy. My Dad used to tell me that Jesus had that gift and so many stories in the Bible will identify that. Dad said, "You have a big responsibility with this gift." I never really knew what that meant until l got older.

In 1995, my Mom told me that she and my Grandma had not spoken for 46 years. My Grandmother Alicia was very protective of my Mom, Luz, and lived a life full of hard work and responsibilities. My Dad was very well-known in Colombia. He owned a radio station and was a singer and dance instructor. He was also known as a ladies' man. When Alicia got wind of the news that he was interested in her daughter, she gave Luz an ultimatum." You have a decision to make; it is either him or me." But my Mom knew she did not really have a choice, she felt such a strong connection to my Dad that there was nothing to think about. My Mom ran away from home to be with my Dad. What she did not realize is that my Grandmother was very serious about her ultimatum and in fact, she *would* be the one who disappeared. What happened was, my Mom did not know where Grandma lived or anything about her for 46 long years.

Here is where my responsibility showed up. Shortly after I was informed of the story, my Angels and Spirit Guides started to get to work. I had no question that it was all in divine order.

One sunny, hot day I was lying on my bed and I heard a voice that said, "Now is the time." I asked, "Now is the time for what?" "Now is the time to connect your Mom with her Mom," said the voice. I asked how, and all I heard was, "Trust that we will show you the way." I knew it was the voice of the Angels. I told my Mom, "We must make a trip to Colombia to find your Mom." She did not hesitate at all, knowing that my strong intention would lead to results. She had already experienced so many proofs of my God-given talent. And of course, my Dad and sister Angela knew for sure that I was being guided by the Angels.

The Angels showed me in advance what my Grandmother's apartment in Colombia looked like and even the street sign. When my Mom, my Dad, Angela and I arrived at that street sign, we saw a church right there. We knew that Grandma must go to this church, so we went inside with the anticipation of finding her. The service was still going on. I remember us looking at every older woman we saw who might resemble my Grandma, even though we had never had a picture of her. My Dad and my sister Angela would say what about that lady or that lady? When church was over, we followed several ladies around outside for a few minutes. Suddenly a peace came over me and I heard a voice say, "Turn here." We did, and that's when I saw the apartment and said with certainty, "This is where she lives."

We were all so very nervous, especially my Dad. We asked a gentleman who had a store downstairs, "Does Alicia live up there?" He said, "Oh yes, Don Alicia is a very sweet lady. Every day she goes to church and always has the rosary in her hand. She hardly eats, though." He asked us who we were, and we said family. He looked very surprised. My Mom knocked on Alicia's door with Angela and me by her side. Alicia opened the door, looked at my Mom and said, "Yes, who are you?" My Mom said, "I am your daughter."
Of course, neither of them recognized each other, because 46 years had gone by. Grandma looked and said, "What! How did you find me?" My Mom replied, "God" and gave her a long hug. Lots of tears were shed.

My Mom introduced me and my sister Angela to our grandmother. "These are my two daughters, Elsa and Angela." Alicia gave us each a kiss and invited us in. She wanted to know all about our lives. When she asked about my Dad, my Mom was shaking. "He is downstairs," she answered, but Grandma did not respond. She looked at me, held my hand and said, "You are an Angel." I did not have any idea why she was telling me that, but I figured I would take advantage of the situation. I asked her if it was possible to allow my Dad to come upstairs. She hesitated but then said "Yes." You could see uncertainty in her face.

I closed the door behind me and looked downstairs. From the outside balcony, I could see my Dad, as nervous as could be. For the first time in my life I saw him as though he was a five- year-old child; he was so scared about what would happen next. This was so different than I was used to seeing my Dad – a very macho, self-confident man everyone respected and was even frightened of. So I went downstairs and told him that Alicia was willing to see him.

"Don't worry. I am going to serenade her with a song," he surprised me by saying. He had a guitar and was confident he would win Grandma over with his great voice. We walked up the stairs and knocked on the door. Grandmother opened the door and Dad started to sing to her. She did not let him finish, but instead grabbed the guitar and threw it on the floor. I thought she was going to slap him. But instead, she threw her arms around him and gave him a big hug. There were tears of love and forgiveness like I had never seen before! I knew the Angels and God had their hands in this.

We were all so excited to have Alicia in our life again. We spent the next four hours with her. The apartment was empty and hardly had any food; it felt very cold. My Dad had me sing her a song as we were getting ready to leave. When I finished she took my hands and said, "I want you to promise me you will do something with your voice." I told her yes, but at that very minute I was telling her that and telling her that I would name my child after her, suddenly I had a vision. I saw Grandma crossing the street and getting run over by a big truck. I even saw the license plate, and how she died instantly. I could not believe I was seeing this in my mind. I thought, WOW!! This could not be true! I tried so hard to erase the vision from my mind.

We all hugged and made an agreement to start communicating every Sunday by phone. Alicia made a comment to my Mom, "Now I can go home" (by home, she meant heaven). My Mom first smiled and did not make much of it. My Mom invited Alicia to come live with us in the U.S. but Alicia was not interested. So we all said a long good-bye and headed back to Florida with such happiness and gratitude for what God had done. We thought everyone will get to meet Grandma on the phone on Sunday. Well, that Sunday never came. On Saturday, Mom received a call that my grandma Alicia had been run over and killed by a big truck. I told her, "Do not tell me anything, Mom. Now let me tell you. Was the license plate ---?" I told her the letters and numbers I had seen in my vision, and I said this is what she was wearing; she had the rosary in her hand and had on her favorite necklace. My Mom said yes, that was all true. I replied, "I am so sorry. I saw this vision and did not tell anyone."

I could not believe what I was seeing, but I truly believe God was showing me the vision to let us all see that this was meant to be. He was saying, I know how hard this is for you to understand, but remember here is your proof that this was meant to happen. This is where the gift of prophecy really shows its responsibility. This made Mom and everyone else feel more at peace with the accident. It is never easy losing your Mom, especially after having 46 years go by, and then you find her and then lose her again. You really have to have a strong connection to God to pull you through this situation.

I encourage you to look at your relationships. If you are having issues with your Mom or Dad, look at the bigger picture and see what a blessing they truly are. I wrote this note for Alicia's eulogy. I call it "Touched by an Angel."

There is a television program called "Touched by an Angel." I never knew that I would experience a touch by an Angel. But Don Alicia Arango, my Grandmother, was just that – an Angel sent from God. When you looked into her eyes, you could see the kindness, the love, and the peace that no words could describe. A touch so soft yet so strong. She carried with her an incredible inner strength that kept her going for so long, although with not much to look forward to, except to see her beautiful daughter Luz. God granted both of them this wish that they had longed for, for so many years.

I thank God for granting me such a blessing to meet her. Her strength I will carry in my heart. Her love I will carry in my soul. For now she is with the Lord, among the other Angels in heaven.

For those of us who did not know her, it is safe to say that she is with us always. Her Spirit will live forever, for this shall never die. Like a shadow on our side, she will be an everlasting Angel shining bright!

Today my Grandma still visits me. She brings me a rosary in the mail when I am getting ready to teach a Mediumship class and always shows me who to give the rosary to. If I am not teaching a class on Mediumship, the rosaries do not come. But then Grandma brings me flowers, beautiful pink roses, through my husband. Although I never really knew her, our short encounter created an everlasting bond. That just goes to show how strong Love is.

Chapter Three
Let Go and Let God

As often as we have all heard this phrase said, "Let go and Let God," it is still a challenge for us to accept.

Why is that? Why do we feel we must have some type of control? Why do we feel if we do not make something happen, it will not happen? Why do we feel we have to please everyone?

These are interesting questions that need to be looked at further if we are to get out of our own way. I will tell you my experiences and realizations as to how I was stopping certain blessings in my life from occurring. Hopefully you will then look at your own life and decide to get out of your own way, to allow your true happiness to come through. I truly believe we are a byproduct of our childhood. If we were not aware that we had a dysfunctional upbringing, we will likely draw that same type of dysfunction into our adult life. We feel we are safe, because this is all we know.

My Dad was such an amazing man. He saw an opportunity to get us out of Colombia and he went for it. However, things did not come easy. He had heard that you can get to the United States by filing an application and taking a test at the Immigration Office. If you were lucky, you got accepted into the United States. He had always known about Florida and how beautiful it was. He believed that there was an opportunity waiting for him on the sunny side of the world. My Dad had a very strong relationship to Mother Mary, and prayed to her often. He always used to tell me never to forget how powerful Mother Mary was, and told me so many incidences where Mother Mary had come to him. Well, this was one of those days. My Dad could not speak English, let alone write English, and one of the prerequisites of passing the test was filling out the English immigration papers. But when he arrived at Immigration, the gentleman at the counter was kind enough to help Dad pass the test! He was so grateful for his prayers being answered, and he came to the U.S. He had now become a resident of the U.S., but the next step was to bring his family over. Once Dad could prove that he had a job and a place to live, he could apply for his family to join him.

My Dad applied and waited patiently for a response. He felt he was not getting anywhere. So, every day for about six months, he would go to the Immigration Office early in the morning and speak to the supervisor. Just shortly after six months passed, the supervisor gave up and told Dad that he would approve our arrival. Dad was just so excited that he wanted to hug the young man, but he would not accept any hugs. My Dad was a very determined man. When he had a vision in his head or a dream, he would stop at nothing to fulfill it. With that said, we all arrived at the airport in Miami on September 25, 1975. The *Miami Herald* had gotten wind of our arrival and was there to greet us and take a picture for the newspaper. Apparently they had never seen such a big family, enough to fill a school bus, arrive from a third-world country with permission to live in the United States.

This was the blessing we had all been waiting for. My Dad and Mom knew this was the land of opportunity, but they also knew they had to work hard to get it.

One of the biggest challenges for them was that in Colombia, everyone had a live-in maid or housekeeper, and with such a big family, we needed two. We all knew and accepted that this was not a luxury we could afford right now. My Dad bought us a two-bedroom, one-bath house with a patio for all of us twelve kids. We shared one room, which was only 10 feet wide by 11 feet long. We had four bunk beds, with two beds on each bunk and one sleeping bag for all nine girls. The boys had to sleep on the open patio and got wet when it rained. Sometimes they would find a spot on the small green couch in the living room.

The closet was small and narrow. The bathroom was extremely small. The toilet practically touched the tub. We had to take turns using the bathroom, and had to wait in line every morning. The older ones always went first. I would get up early sometimes just to make sure I was not rushed, but someone always beat me to it. I suffered all of my life from constipation because I never had time to go, since I was always being pushed out.

We also had an uninvited guest who lived in the house. Every night I would see this big ghost. He was about six feet seven inches, and looked like a bodybuilder. He would just stand at the edge of the bed, with his hands folded. He had blonde hair and what seemed to be blue eyes. Every night I would cry myself to sleep; we had to sleep head-to-toe to make room for the other person. I would pinch my older sister Nora, who used to sleep with me, when I saw the ghost, but she never felt the pinch. So I would cry myself to sleep. This was before I started talking to ghosts and allowing the deceased to give me messages.

I remember one night I got so fed up, I screamed "GET OUT!!!" to the big ghost. He looked like something out of a movie. His transparent body turned to blue and slid right out the bottom of the door. When I got older, I found out that my older sisters had seen the ghost and, of course, my father would tell the ghost to leave all the time.

My Dad was a very popular singer, radio broadcaster and dance instructor in Colombia. So when he got to the United States, he always had that dream inside of him, to make it big here. But with so many children to feed and such big responsibilities, his goal was primarily to keep us safe and have a steady income. Oftentimes my Dad had to go to the movie theater to get some sleep. He said that is where he had the most peace.

My Dad was very strict with all of us. We were not

given the choice of speaking freely; we could only speak if we were asked to. I consider this to be a dysfunction, and encourage parents to let their children speak.

When you grow up with a parent who is physically or mentally abusive, you tend to have low self-esteem. You feel it is somehow your fault, and since my Dad would drink sometimes to hide from his problem, he would later realize what he had done and say he was sorry. But that does not take away the pain and the feeling that you do not deserve anything good in your life.

Then as you grow up, you draw to yourself that same type of relationship. We grow up wanting to control everyone and wanting everyone to like us, because again, that is a byproduct of our childhood. But when we realize what we don't want and realize what we do deserve, then we will draw to ourselves someone who is healthy. It starts with letting go and letting God, surrendering to the Higher Power, but first recognizing the power you have to change your belief system about yourself and the world.

The Angel created for me a healing technique that helped me. It is called Emotional Replacement Therapy™, a healing technique that takes you back to your mother's womb. It replaces everything that ever impacted you in a negative way and created a bad imprint in your energy field with a positive energy that does serve you.

One day I was lying on my bed and I heard a voice

that said, "Heal yourself." I was very open to the guidance I was about to receive and asked, "What do I need to heal?" The voice said, "You have control issues." I was so surprised to hear this, since I was not aware and it was not something I was willing to look at before.

I asked, "What do you want me to do?" The voice said, "Go back into your mother's womb and you will be guided." Although I had no idea as to how I would do that, I just trusted in Spirit and knew something profound was about to happen. I closed my eyes, took a deep breath, and started to channel the messages from my Angels. I saw my etheric body next to me, guiding me through the healing process.

Imagine for a moment that you have a Double in front of you. My Double was guiding me back into my mother's womb, taking me back, all the way back to when I was not even born yet. Then I could see myself bundled up in that very safe, warm place. I was happy, but I could see there were issues going on outside of my mom's womb. I was instructed to look through her stomach and see what was going on. My mom was very sad; she had been fighting with my Dad, and she was bedridden because she was so emotionally upset.

The doctor said that I was a miracle, because every time my Mom would get upset, she would lose a lot of blood. She was on bed rest with me for over six months! My Mom prayed constantly for my survival, and was as determined to have me as I was determined to come out. I could feel her desire and her love. This gave me even more strength to come through.

There was a big celebration in my Mom's heart and I could feel this. She never gave up on me and felt so happy that I made it. Now I am being guided by my Double. What happened when you were twelve years old, since she is taking me back to this year? All I could remember is what I looked like and my throat being shut. I told her, "It is hard for me to speak." What is happening? She asked, and I said, "My Dad is controlling me, not allowing me to speak." Then she said, "So is that why you are controlling your husband, because you didn't have a voice?" You were controlled then, and now you feel you have to control?" I said, "WHAT?"

Wow, I had opened my eyes to a transformation I had no idea was coming. "Are you ready to change the scene in your head?" my Double asked, and I said, "Yes." She responded, "Visualize yourself when you were twelve years old, with your Dad in front of you, encouraging you to speak. He is not controlling you, and you are free to be you." I imagined this in my head and changed the picture in my mind, on a DNA level. When the healing session was over, I felt so free and light. I just knew that things would be different. Now I do not try to control anything, and I know that I am different. I am so grateful that the Spirits have manifested this healing for me.

I currently teach this method of healing in my

workshops.

I am not saying you have to do this in order for you to heal from a situation, but this is a healing technique that worked for me and other clients who have come to see me. It is quite powerful. I totally believe in the Angels and trust them to the fullest. I am so grateful for all the wonderful things my Dad did for me, and now I only remember the good. That is a wonderful energy to hold. I no longer hold any resentment, anger or anything negative in my blueprint or in my energy field. It is almost like rewriting your life story. It is a big blessing. I also know my Dad was a byproduct of his upbringing, and this is what is so fascinating-- you see things the way you should, in the light, always. This healing showed me how to let go and let God. I also did not have the need to please everyone so they would like me, because I like me. There are so many healing levels to it.

"Be Beautiful Inside"

My Daddy use to tell me be Beautiful inside,
you are too young now, but one day you will realize.

My Daddy use to hold me and rock me to a tune,
he always told me, darling be careful with all that you
do.

My Daddy use to hold me and sit me on his lap, he often
told me, "You are so beautiful, do you know that?"

He said you are too young now, but love is all that's
real; give your life to love and how good it makes you
feel.

Keep your heart steadfast and keep it pure, love is
what you will find, it will last and it will endure.

There are many Beautiful people with blue or green
eyes, but there is nothing more important than to be
beautiful inside. There is nothing more
important than to be Beautiful inside!

Elsa J. Stokes, © Copyright 2009

Chapter Four
Soul Mates

A soul mate is someone you feel you are connected with on a spiritual level. This is someone you know you have had a past life with, and you are coming together to continue to learn and grow from each other.

I have heard that you have very few soul mates in each lifetime. But I would have to say this is not my experience.

I have had many soul mates, and what is so unique is that God always shows me what is going to happen before it does. It was the same when it came to meeting boyfriends.

I always knew who I would meet, when I would meet him and how long the relationship would last. One time I actually gave God the name of the guy I wanted to meet and described what he looked like. God showed me where I would meet him, and that I would be his girl by the end of that night. I had never met him before, but I met him on a soul level. I could see what he looked like and I knew his first and last name. Spirit gave me this. It never ceases to amaze me what Spirit can do!

I told my best friend at the time to come along to see what God can do. I told her exactly what would happen and she was so interested, she had to see it for herself. Needless to say, she never doubted me again.

Living my life like this was not easy, but that is all I knew. I was so fascinated to see that every vision I had would come true.

I made an agreement with God as far as my husband was concerned. I asked Him not to show me the face of the man I was going to marry. I really wanted this to be a surprise. Well, God has a very funny sense of humor, because in 1995 I remember seeing a TV broadcast saying that the designer Versace had been murdered. Carey Stokes was one of the models they interviewed about Versace's death.

I was watching TV with my sister Angela and when Carey came on the screen, I said to her, "I want to marry that man." She laughed, and then I said, "I am going to marry that man." She replied, "How are you going to do that? He lives in Arizona." "I don't know. I just know I am going to marry that man."

More than 10 years went by and I had forgotten all about that. When I met Carey at a restaurant bar I was with my sister Angela, my brothers and some friends. I saw Carey from afar and said, "That guy looks like Arnold Schwarzenegger," and pointed to him. He saw me pointing and came over. "Hi. I saw you pointing at me." "Yes, you look so much like Arnold Schwarzenegger." He laughed, asked me for my business card and said, "Maybe we will get a dance later." I said sure, but he never got a chance because I was always dancing with someone else.

A few days went by, he called, and we went out. And the funny part is two months before I met him; I kept seeing a white couch and a golden retriever. I would see myself driving to his house, but all Spirit would show me was the couch and the dog. God said "This is the man you will marry." So when I stepped foot into Carrey's house there they were; the couch and the dog. I was breathless, but did not dare say anything. I did not want him to get scared and run away. After all, it had only been a week or so we had been going

out.

Just over two years went by. Carey told me he heard the voice of God. It woke him up and said, "You have to marry her. Marry her now." He sat up, went directly to the store and proposed that night.

I never really wanted to tell him of my gifts but they were getting harder and harder to hide.

One day he had gone out with his friend. He told me he was going to Miami and about the plans he had made. The next day I asked him, "How was Boca? I saw you went to Boca and hung out with some girls." I told him the color of one

girl's dress was red, and what they had in their hands. "I saw that you behaved. Did you have a good time?" He was speechless, hung up the phone, and called his friend to tell him what I had said. His friend said, "Dude, she's having you followed."

I was not trying to check up on him, Spirit just took me there. I had no control; in fact, I had to ask Spirit to get me out of there as I wanted to be where I was, not where he was. Ever since he knew I was not like the other girls he had dated.

Carey is definitely my soul mate and I know we have been together many lifetimes and will be together in future life-times. I have done destiny retrieval and saw that we are together in the life time to come.

Now that we are married, Spirit sometimes takes me to where he is and then I have to ask Spirit to bring me back. So God kept his promise. He had me forget the first time I saw him and the message I got. He didn't show me Carey's face, just the couch and the dog.

I have heard so many people say they want to meet their soul mate and are waiting around for it to happen. I know that when you pray, God hears your prayer. I also have to say that we sometimes limit ourselves as to what we will allow and not allow in our life.

If I had not been open to dating a man that had a child, I would not have experienced the blessing that has been. I fell in love with Carrey's son Dillon at first sight. Be open to what God wants for you, to what Spirit wants for you.

Also be open to dating someone when you may feel you don't have a connection, or maybe you feel the relationship is new, because this just might be the beginning of you and your soul mate. Open yourself up on all levels. Allow yourself to receive, and know that you deserve to be in a healthy, happy relationship. Carry yourself as if you are worth your weight in gold, not in an ego-centered way but in a surety that expresses your love for yourself.

Chapter Five
The Power of Prayer

It has been said that there is nothing more powerful than prayer. Something magical, mystical and out of the ordinary happens when we pray. We find ourselves in a vulnerable state. We recognize that certain things are out of our control. We surrender to a higher power. We understand and appreciate life more. We make a magical connection.

Praying allows us to really let go and let God. We are putting our faith, trust and hope in a divine higher source. It takes us out of fear, out of the ego and into the heart. When we pray, our heart chakra is open and stimulated. We feel love for the universe, for others, and for ourselves. We connect to that source that is pure love, pure light. We know that we are being heard and being held, and something magical happens, like when we are holding a child or when we are being held as a child. We know we are loved and being held or supported in some way, and that somehow everything will work itself out. We open our heart to miracles. We are receptive to receiving, which is true manifestation at work. So pray for someone today. Pray for the planet, the earth, the animals, the children. Pray for yourself. It is one of the least selfish things you can do. When you pray for yourself, it will help you and affect everyone around you. When you are good, all things flow to you and you can help others.

So many times I have heard people say; I pray for others but hardly pray for myself. They feel that praying for themselves is a selfish act. This could not be further from the truth. We must first love and take care of ourselves in order to truly be there for someone else. This is why when you travel on an airplane, you are told to put the mask on yourself before you put it on your child. We are number one, or at most number two, after God. But we are the ones we have to love first.

I have so many answered prayers that it is hard to remember them all, but I can tell you one that happened many years ago that I will never forget.

As I told you before, I came from a family of twelve (eight sisters and three brothers). I will not disclose my family name to keep it as anonymous as possible. One of my sisters had been missing for five years. No one knew what had happened to her. Every day I would pray to God to bring her back. I had a vision that I would see her at a bus stop on my way to a job interview. At the time I had this vision, my Mom and Dad had gone to Jerusalem, to the Wailing Wall, where they had written their prayer to find their daughter on a piece of paper and put it into the crack in the wall. It has been said that the Divine presence continues to reside at the Wailing Wall. Thus, praying there is like praying directly to God. Originally called simply the Western Wall, it acquired the name Wailing Wall because of the nature of the prayers spoken and written there.

My Mom and Dad went there to pray for a miracle to find their missing daughter in 1995. And, as fate would have it, the next afternoon after my vision the entire incident came true, except Spirits did not show me what would happen when I saw her.

I was driving to my interview. It was like any other day; the sun was shining brightly; a few clouds were overhead. The temperature was quite muggy, though bearable. I looked over to the left and saw my long-lost sister standing in front of a bus bench with ragged jeans and t-shirt and a dollar bill in her hand, waiting patiently for the bus. This was in Hollywood, Florida. I quickly made a U-turn when I realized that my eyes were not playing tricks on me. I stopped the car, ran over and called out her name. I was so excited to see her. She looked at me and said, "Who are you? I do not know you." I said, "What are you talking about? I am your sister." She had a stony face and replied, "I have never seen you in my life. Excuse me, lady, but you are making me uncomfortable."

I was in a state of shock; first, that I had found my sister and second, that she was acting as if she didn't know me. I could see the bus coming from a distance. I really did not know what to do. How could I prove to her that I was her sister? I knew she knew I was her sister, but did not want to be discovered. The bus slowly approached and I pleaded with her, "Please don't get on the bus," as I grabbed her arm. "I love you, and I am your sister." "Let go of me," she said and ran onto the bus. I watched it slowly drive away, with tears rolling down my face. I cannot imagine that she denied she knew her own sister.

My interview was in five minutes and I had to get to my scheduled obligation. I wiped away my tears, composed myself and walked into the interview as if nothing had happened. The interview went well, but I decided against taking the job.

On my way home I started to think how I could find my sister. I know she must live in Hollywood. A voice told me to put a request in the newspaper. Someone would surely see the notice and mention it to her.

My parents were just heading home that night from Jerusalem, after much determination and prayer to find their missing daughter. I called and told them what had happened. They were so happy to hear that she was alive and well, and continued to pray that God would bring her back to the family.

The following morning I called the *Sun Sentinel* and told them my story. A reporter came to my house that evening. My sister's daughter and other family members were there to give insights as to how the family was feeling about the situation. The article ran on the front page of the *Miami Herald* and the *Sun Sentinel* with the title "You do not mistake your own sister."

Well, my "missing" sister read the newspaper article, and was so mad; she called my parents to tell them how upset she was. Long story short, everyone made up and my sister is now a part of the family again. Everyone was so excited to have her with us again!

God is an awesome God. He answers prayers in his own time. Sometimes we have to be patient. Never stop praying for what you want. Never give up hope, and always have faith that everything works out for the best.

Chapter Six

God Shows the Way

God somehow always shows us the way in life; He gives us signs and signals as to what to do. It is such a blessing when God shows you the way for someone else, when He makes it clear to you what your role is in helping someone else. You know you have no other choice; you must do what you are told. I believe God has certain people bless other people. I also believe that many things in life are already destined. The reason I believe this is because time and time again, I have not been able to change a vision I have seen. One particular vision was a very pleasant one and will stay with me for a long time.

When I was about 25 years old, I was with my partner at a high school football game. When the game was over, he started walking toward a friend of his who was on the field. His friend was about twenty feet away from us; we started walking toward his friend. From a distance I could see his friend, but could not make out his face. As he started to walk closer, I also saw my sister Nelly with four kids walking toward me.

I asked my partner, "Who is that man coming toward us?" He said, "Ah, that guy's name is Jim," and I said, "We have to introduce him to my sister Nelly." My partner laughed, "Are you crazy? Jim is only twenty-two years old; your sister is thirty." I insisted, "Do not question me, just do it, please," and he said okay.

As Jim and I were introduced, my partner asked, "Would you like to meet Elsa's sister?" Jim replied, "If she looks anything like her, yes!" So that night I told my sister Nelly to come along with us to watch a movie. We told her about Jim, but she was not interested in him. But she went with us anyway because we were going to see a movie she wanted to see. We all met at the movie theater. The movie was good. On the way out, Jim asked Nelly if he could get some ice cream and take her home afterwards. She said yes.

The next day I asked Nelly how it went. She said, "He is very nice, but I am not interested. He had me up for hours. He is a Catholic and I am a born-again Christian. Plus, he is way too young. He's a baby, and I do not want to go out with a baby."

Well, as Spirit would have it, while I was at Nelly's house, Jim called and I answered. Nelly would prompt me to say she was not there and I would say, "Sure, hold on, she's right here." She would get so mad at me! I would just laugh, because I knew it was all God's plan. Well, before you know it, three months went by and they were talking marriage. He said that the minute he met her, he knew he wanted to marry her. They now actually have those four children that I saw walking next to him at the football field the first night I met him.

Another thing happened with Nelly. She was pregnant and expecting to have a baby boy. I was driving on the expressway one day and Spirit decided to show me what was going to happen with the birth. I could not see any cars in front of me. Spirit showed me Nelly having the baby and at what time. There was a big clock with the hands pointing to 6. I was so excited when I came back from the vision. I realized where I was, and got off at the first exit to call Nelly and tell her the great news. She started laughing and said, "Elsa, you are so funny. I do not even have any labor pains yet. How could I have the baby at that time?" Ten minutes after we hung up, her labor pains started. She went to the hospital and had the baby exactly at 6 o'clock, just as God had shown me.

I was very pleased to have had this vision because everything was positive and beautiful. I am very grateful when things like this happen.

Be open to receiving messages. I believe we are always getting messages. We may not get them as clear as this, but just know that there are always signs along the way. All we have to do is be open and aware of them and most importantly, be willing to listen because sometimes the message will be in a form of a voice.

Chapter Seven
Manifestation

Ever wonder why it is so easy for some people to manifest something just by thinking of it? And why others try so hard and cannot seem to manifest anything they want in their life?

Manifestation means aligning your wants, your thoughts and your heart to the all-powerful energy of God, of creation.

If we complain or feel like a victim, that stops manifesting in its tracks. We have to be clear about what we want, when we want it, why we want it and how bad we want it (or, should I say, how good we want it).

At this very moment, we are manifesting. The question is; are we manifesting what we want or what we don't want?

In order to open up to the world of magic and miracles, we recognize that our thoughts, beliefs and behaviors play a key role in the manifestation process.

We all have the capacity and the power to manifest our deepest desires. We simply have to look at the rules that govern manifestation.

Imagination is the muscle behind all manifestation. We must first imagine what we want; taste it, feel it, touch it, see it, and know it. Remember when we were children? We never had a problem imagining toys to play with, or different scenarios for our childhood adventures. We did not know what life was like without imagination.

Now we are being called to live in this place of imagination in our adult life. Imagination is our best friend, for you can only create what you first imagine. Our miracles are waiting to be manifested. Intention follows imagination. Combining them, we guide the powerful energies of love toward healing and manifestation. However, visualization is the power to create a new reality by harnessing the power of our imagination.

Another key role of manifestation is our intention. So if imagination and intention equals manifestation, what is the driving force for our intention? Intention is an act of faith, an understanding of our knowing what it takes to make something happen. How do we fuel our body, mind and spirit to have intention? We have to be clear of our desire. Once our thoughts are created and there is an emotion tied to this creation, a signal will be created to vibrate your intention. We will draw the same vibration back to ourselves that we are sending out.

Intention is all about paying attention to details. We recognize that intention is the blueprint for manifesting change, and that details are what make up that blueprint.

Visualize, will, action, faith, enthusiasm. The more enthusiasm and faith you are able to put into your picture, the sooner it will come into visible form. One way to keep your enthusiasm strong and increasing is by keeping your intention a secret. The moment you speak about it, it loses its power and becomes weaker. Your power, your magnet of attraction, is weakened and consequently cannot reach very far. Write it down, talk it over with yourself, but keep it hush-hush it is a secret, unless you are going to ask someone to help you manifest it or to join you in prayer. This must be someone you can trust. This must be someone who is spiritual who understands how delicate the situation is and will keep it a secret.

I would like to tell you a story of a true manifestation at work. My sister, who was trying to get pregnant for many years, came to me. "Elsa, please help me," she said. "I have been trying to get pregnant, but nothing is working. I am going to a specialist and still no success." I asked my guides what I should do and heard a clear voice: "See what is going on with her ovaries." I do consider myself a medical intuitive, I can clearly see what is going on in someone's body, mind or spirit. I truly believe some of us are just born with this gift.

As she lay down and I placed my hands over her ovaries, I could see there was some energy blocking her ovaries from producing a baby. It was evident to me that her ex-husband was wrapped tightly around her ovaries, preventing her from bearing a child with her new husband. I told her what I saw and asked her permission to remove her ex-husband. She could not say yes fast enough. I removed him with the help of Spirit and then started to "repair" her ovaries, preparing them for this wonderful journey of becoming a proud Mom. When we were done, I heard a voice saying, "Now you must manifest the child." We went through a manifestation meditation that I will go over toward the end of this chapter, sent our prayers and an intention to God and the Angels, and let them go to work.

A week later my sister came to me and asked if she was pregnant, because she felt something. I put my hand on her belly and started to cry. I told her, "Oh my gosh, this baby is so beautiful. It is a boy and he has our Brother Gabriel's spirit. He is a crystal child." I could see what this baby looked like, his personality and how he loved the beach. Spirit showed me scenes of him with his father, playing ball when he was about two years old. I hugged her and said, "I am so happy for you." My sister also had tears in her eyes.

We waited to get the official news that she was in fact pregnant. When he was born, I think I cried even more than she did from the miracle of this beautiful baby boy. My sister was over forty when he was born. And I am so proud she asked me to be his Godmother.

He is now just over two years old, learning to play ball with his father, and, yes, he goes crazy over the sand and the ocean. This is an example of manifestation at its best.

I believe when we want something we have to ask for it and then be patient and wait for the Divine to give it to us.

I always like to say, be careful what you want to manifest, because you are indeed powerful enough to get it.

Meditation Technique

Visualize two white cords going down from your ankles, all the way down to the ground, until you see two red boulders. Anchor these white cords on the boulders. Now visualize beautiful gold energy coming up the cords. Allow this golden energy to travel all the way up to the top of your head. Now visualize a big ball on the top of your head. Make this ball whatever color you like. It is a see-through ball.

Now place yourself and what you want to manifest at this time in the transparent ball. Visualize yourself inside the colored ball. Visualize what it is you want. Now allow the ball to roll down from your crown chakra (the top of your head). Let it roll down your third eye, the area between your eyebrows, down to your throat chakra, down to your heart chakra, down to your stomach, to your belly button. Now, let it come out of your belly button, creating it once again.

What does your gut feel about this manifestation? Let the feeling go upwards. How does your heart feel about this? How happy are you? Keep going up to the throat, what does it sound like? Go up to the third eye; what does it look like? Take a good look at the ball. Let it travel up over your head. Now put your hands on the ball and say, "I give this to you, God, Angels," or whomever you want to give it to, release the ball to the heavens. Then wait for its return.

After you have done this manifestation, make sure you are in a receiving energy. Know that you deserve this, and that it is your birthright. If it is your desire, God gave you that desire. As long as your manifestation is for the good and does not harm anyone, then you are deserving of it. Make sure you have forgiven yourself for anything you feel you have done wrong, and also forgive others whom have done you wrong.

Too many times I have seen people who are trying to manifest things in their life, but they are still holding onto resentment, anger, blame, shame and unworthiness. We have to clean up the river so the water can flow easily.

Chapter Eight
Look to the Light

As I was meditating today, I was reminded of the Light that entered my life yesterday. My day was going along just like any ordinary day. I had just finished visiting my favorite spa. While I was driving away, I saw a man who looked like my deceased brother Mario walking alongside my car. I instantly felt sorrow and thought wow, how could someone resemble someone else so closely. I tried to brush off the sadness because I had to go to Office Max and get some supplies for an upcoming workshop.

When I was almost ready to leave the store, I heard a voice saying, "Look at the cameras." Lo and behold, the camera that I wanted was on sale. Excitedly, I asked for assistance. Well, that camera was sold out; the salesperson was trying to see if he could get some from another store or on back-order. While I was waiting around, it was closing time, I again saw this guy who looked so much like Mario, but this time when he was younger, in his 30s. I looked at him, but he did not notice. I thought, now this is unbelievable, I am being shown my brother again. It took everything I had not to cry and make a scene. This guy was so full of life and so vibrant; he seemed to have similar energy to my late brother Mario.

It was past closing time and the gentleman who was trying to help me said that there was nothing more they could do. He asked me to come back or call on Friday. I was walking out the door, when who was in front of me, the young vibrant man. He looked at me, said hello and smiled from ear to ear. I was so affected by this; it took me a while to drive away. I had to wipe away my tears. I knew my brother was trying to send a message to me, but I was not sure what it was. I felt his love and knew he would come back and talk to me.

The next morning while I was in meditation, I heard Mario's voice. "I showed you these gentlemen to let you know I was all right and happy. I know you think of me and feel sorry for all the suffering I went through while I was battling the cancer. Please do not feel bad for me. God is so amazing; he made me forget the pain. This is how we should live our life; replace the suffering with Love, vibrant Light and Joy. See the light in everyone; we are all part of this invisible light. Remember, life is meant to be enjoyed and celebrated. We are always celebrating and singing here.

"We are sending light to the world. Focus; keep your eyes on the light, for it is as real as your fingers. You hold beautiful light in your hands, in your body. Concentrate on this light every day. Ask the Holy Spirit to fill you with this light daily, and you will see how you will live more in the flow. Make this a part of your daily prayer and meditation: " God, fill me with your light. Fill me with your love. Fill me with your joy. For you alone, God, only you can illuminate my light.' I showed you my light; now go into the world and show yours. I love you." What a powerful, beautiful message I got from my brother!

The next day, the Angels brought me my camera. I saw a vision of what store it would be at, it was at Office Depot not Office Max. I called the store and they said yes, we have it, even in my favorite color. So the delay at the store around my camera had been divinely ordered in order for me to see the vibrant young man who resembled Mario. God is so amazing!

Everything in life is so divinely ordered. If we just take a moment to realize that, we would appreciate our blessings every day.

Chapter Nine
Surrender and Release

As I sit here to write this chapter, I am reminded of the power of serenity. When I surrender to a higher force and let go of control, then, and only then, will my writing flow. I am left with a feeling of contentment that everything happens in divine order. We cannot push, rush or make things happen before they are meant to. Sometimes in life the biggest lesson is just to wait. Wait on the calling from your Guides and your Angels.

Sometimes we think we have it all planned out. I am going to do this in the morning, this in the afternoon, and this in the evening. And then something will happen to turn everything upside down.

This happened to me one day when I had back-to-back appointments. I got the pull from my Angels to call my Mom, who was with my sister Irene. I asked them to come over, since I had about forty-five minutes before my next session. My Mom walked in the door looking very fragile. I told her I would be glad to do a healing. She was open to the idea, but needed to take a nap before I started. Usually she takes a twenty minute nap, but she had not slept for two days and did not look good. Irene and I went into my room while Mom took her nap.

Then the Angels guided me to assist my sister. We started talking about a current situation she was in. Half an hour went by and Mom had not knocked on the door yet. The last thing I wanted to do was wake her up; she looked like she really needed her rest.

I was very aware of the time, and grateful that the next session that I had would be on the phone. But I surrendered to my Higher Source and asked, "What do you want me to do?" Source said to reschedule the phone healing session. So I did, and not even a minute later, I heard a voice say, "Heal your sister." She and I started working, and it was so obvious that my sister really needed the healing.

I was working with my sister for over two hours, with no sign of my Mom. She was also being guided, because instead of her interrupting us, she went into another room, started praying the rosary, and then was drawn to a spiritual book I had. When she came in later, she was like a little girl, as happy as can be, without a care in the world. God was healing her while I was healing my sister; and, of course, the pleasure and reward was all mine.

With so much to do in my mind, Spirits make time stand still and make us listen while they are directing. Spirit knows who needs what, and when. I find this happening to me often. Sometimes I even have to change my appointments around to fit the Angels' requests.

I am grateful when this happens, because the biggest healing for me is to surrender and release. I get all the blessings when this happens. I then have a peace beyond understanding. I believe the key to happiness and contentment is releasing our control to a higher force. When we are constantly connected to our Angels and Guides, life flows like a river, with only little ripples along the way.

"Like *water which can clearly mirror the sky and the trees only so long as its surface is undisturbed, the mind can only reflect the true image of the self when it is tranquil and wholly relaxed.*" – Indra Devi, yoga master

Chapter Ten

The Dark Forces

This is a subject no one likes to discuss or acknowledge. I never like talking about the dark forces and I was always told that if I did not believe in them, then nothing would happen to me. However, as I got older and went through shamanic training, I came to realize this was not true. These forces were real, but there were things you could do to protect yourself against them. I will go over some protection techniques at the end of this chapter.

These stories that I am about to disclose to you are real-life stories that I saw experienced or heard of.

The first story is about my Dad. When I was still living with my parents, my Dad had the most profound experience. I can remember the story as if it was yesterday. One day my parents decided to go to sleep earlier than usual. We children were all in our rooms, getting ready to go into dream-time.

The following morning, Dad told me this story. He even woke up early to make sure he got a chance to talk to me before I headed to work. He started, "You are not going to believe what happened to me last night." I said, "What?" He replied, "An evil spirit entered me and told me to strangle your Mom." I was so shocked at what I was hearing him say, I told Dad to slow down and tell me all about it.

"I was getting ready to go to bed; your Mom was already asleep. I could hear her sleeping very peacefully. I gave her a kiss on the cheek and was reflecting on what a beautiful and special wife I had. Not even a few seconds later, I looked to my right and saw a dark figure. I could not make it out, but I felt it enter my body. I thought to myself, what was that? Then all of a sudden, I heard a voice saying, 'Strangle your wife, and choke her to death.' I felt very strange; I did not feel like myself! This voice kept telling me to strangle her. I got closer to her neck and felt I had no control over my hands. Part of me really wanted to strangle her! Then it felt like a light bulb went on and I realized what I was about to do. The last thing in the world I wanted was to hurt my adorable wife, the most important person in my life. I said, "NO" out loud, but still I kept hearing this voice.

"Then I called on Mother Mary to come and help me.

"Virgin Mary, you have always been there for me in the past. I am asking for your help, as I feel I have no control over my body, especially my hands. Please save me, help me, I beg of you." Then not a moment later, I saw a huge white light in front of me and what appeared to be Mother Mary. She had a big sword in her hand and cut me open, right below my right rib cage. I could see this evil Spirit come out of me. It looked like a monster, stared at me and made a very ugly, loud noise. I was not dreaming this, because I had not even laid down to rest my eyes. Mother Mary closed my cut skin with her hand and sent me white light that had a golden glow. I woke up this morning and realized I had the scar to prove this had happened. Look, here is my scar!"

I was speechless, and thought to myself, Dad has gone mad. But then I heard a voice saying, "He is telling the truth; this really did happen." It wasn't that I didn't believe him. But how could something this crazy happen to anyone
I know, let alone my own Dad? I knew he was eccentric, but this was over the top!

The next story I am about to tell you happened to me. We were not living in the same house as when we first arrived in Miami. My Dad had bought the house next door and added three bedrooms to make sure we would all be very comfortable. So now our home had six bedrooms and two bathrooms. Also, the ghost that haunted us in the other house did not bother us in the new house.

I was getting ready for sleep one night and just before I closed my eyes, I saw a ghost in front of me. Not only was she in front of me, she was actually on top of me. The ghost was a black woman wearing a police uniform. She was very strong, with wide shoulders and big legs. She placed my hands on top of my head and said menacingly, "I am going to rape you now." I tried to pull her off me, but I couldn't. I cried, "No, Stop, Stop." Then I heard a voice say "Pray to Jesus. He will save you." So I started praying the Our Father prayer. She started to fade away until she was completely gone. I have never been so scared in all of my life.

I knew then how important it was to have a relationship with such a powerful force that was a clear representation of Light and Love. I was so grateful that my Mom and Dad took us to church every Sunday, and that Jesus was there to protect me.

I have had other instances that happened to me, where I felt there was a hand on my hip or on my side. Then I prayed and asked Jesus to help me and the feeling left me. I can understand how hard it is to believe that this could happen, but not until you experience it yourself can you really describe how real it is.

This story happened to one of the clients who came to me for healing work. Prior to her arrival, I knew that she needed to have something extracted, but nothing could prepare me to experience what I experienced.

In the shamanic work that I do, it is not uncommon to see that there are unwanted entities inside someone's body, either an entity or crystallized energy or an emotional energy that is interfering with a person's well-being.

I got a call from a client who wanted to come in and see me. I always check with my Angels to make sure I am supposed to work with this person. Then I heard in a clear voice, "Give this client to your husband. Have him do the healing work." I told her I thought it was best if my husband worked with her first, and then we could make an appointment for another time. She was open to the idea and was very anxious to have a healing.

The day she arrived, I introduced myself and my husband. She did not speak perfect English, but she understood enough to get by. She was a beautiful Latin girl going through severe depression and had made several attempts to kill herself. I closed the door behind me but something told me not to go very far. So I went to a nearby drugstore, only a block away, to pick up a few items. Within ten minutes, my husband sent me a text and said, "Please come now. I need your help." I rushed there without hesitation.

When I opened the door, I could see my husband performing an exorcism. I quickly came inside and started to help. I called on Jesus and Mother Mary, and started speaking in tongues. This entity did not have a choice; it was being guided to come out. When it finally left her body, she fell back into my arms, completely relaxed. I could see this energy, the Spirit that had made a home in her body for over five years, very upset that it was being pushed to get out. The entity had a monster-like image. I really could not figure out the image, but it was very dark in nature. As it was being pulled out, it was fighting to stay in her body. She went into convulsions and was saying things she herself did not understand.

I knew the Angels wanted to protect me and had sent my husband to do the job because he is stronger and taller than me. The girl was small, almost my weight and my height, but Carey said that her energy was so strong, it almost knocked him down. I was there at the time Spirit wanted me. She left there a different person. She could not stop crying from the joy she had in her heart. But she was crying tears of happiness. Spirit told me to look at her and say, "Look at yourself, You are so beautiful." She went to a nearby mirror, let her hair down and said, "Yes, I am beautiful." Part of the reason she wanted to kill herself was that she felt ugly. But she was not ugly; the Spirit inside of her was ugly.

My husband and I have seen so many cases where people lose the essence of who they are and their life purpose because an evil entity has entered their body. I know no one wants to acknowledge that this sort of thing exists, but it is best to protect yourself.

Here is a protection technique you can use: You might feel that you have never experienced any dark forces, and I really do not want to put any fear into you. This does not happen to everyone; you can go your entire life and not experience these entities. But what I do know is that they are attracted to lower energies, so if you are drinking, or doing drugs, they feed off that. However, you do not need to be doing either of those activities, and they still could show up in your life.

Protection Meditation:

Do this meditation while you are sitting down, lying down or in a yoga pose. Take three cleansing breaths, in and out. Allow yourself to relax. Visualize a white light coming from below your feet. Visualize the white light coming up your body, going all through your body, up to 15 inches above the top of your head. Then say this prayer: Angels divine, down ray golden light in my energy centers, wrap me in your protective light. Now visualize the white light above your head turning gold, and see a big ball of gold energy entering your body. The energy is all around you, 15 feet in all directions, almost as if though you are inside the ball of light. Allow this energy to pay special attention to your third eye, your throat, your heart, and your stomach area.

Visualize this ball, this gold ball of light, spinning clockwise in all of these areas. Go down with this ball of light, all the way down the body, to the bottom of your feet. When you get to the bottom of your feet, inhale this golden light. Hold your breath and visualize the golden light expand your body into seven layers all around you. The Angels will now wrap you in their layer of protection. Archangel Michael is especially good for protection.

Archangel Michael, keep me protected at all times. I am forever grateful for this protection. This is just one of many protection techniques. Taking a spiritual protection class is extremely beneficial, if you are called to do so.

71

Chapter Eleven

New Heart

Today I gave myself a new heart. A heart that is free to love, a heart that has no past wounds or negative memories. I forgive all those who have hurt me. I forgive myself for anything I feel I have done wrong. I give myself a new body, a new start, a new life, a new beginning.

Some people think that forgiveness is a sign of weakness, but it is really a sign of strength. The more you can forgive and the sooner you can forgive, the stronger you become and the closer you get to Source.

Our true goals and happiness begins with forgiving ourselves; if we cannot forgive ourselves, then we cannot forgive anyone else. We may think we have forgiven them, but there is that hidden little piece inside us that is still holding on to shame, pain and resentment.

Why is it that the past stays in the present? Why do we keep bringing to the surface what has been washed away on the shore? Why do we torture ourselves this way?

Did you know that bones become stronger when they are broken? Well, the same is true with relationships. Your relationships become stronger when there is forgiveness and reconciliation. Forgiveness means feeling and acting as if the affront had never occurred. This is when you know true forgiveness has taken place.

If you have never traveled into the underworld before, then do not worry if you cannot do this meditation. In shamanic training, you learn how to go into the underworld; or, maybe you have taken a workshop or have listened to a CD that guides you there. You will know how to go to the underworld since you have done it before. This was given to me by my Angels. It is a form of psychic surgery in the underworld; I never learned this in shamanic training. I believe it is a gift handed down from Spirit, to be able to do psychic surgery. Since you are doing this through the Angels energy and through my energy, then the healing process will take place, because Spirits have already agreed this healing to be true. However, I have also included an Angelic Meditation that you might feel more comfortable doing.

A simple way to forgive, that will have you feeling refreshed and new, is to first write a letter to the Creator, or God, stating everything, and everyone, you can think of that have hurt you. Pick up that letter and get ready to journey into the underworld. Take a stone, blow on it three times, and let all your intention goes to the stone. Now place the stone on the chakra that you feel has been most affected by hurt. If you do not know for sure, you can take a pendulum and run the energy by testing your chakras. If the pendulum is spinning counter-clockwise and reaches the lowest of the chakras, this is where you place the stone. Take your hand, a rattle or a feather and spin it counter-clockwise for ten seconds; place the stone there. Close your eyes, take three cleansing breaths, relax, and allow yourself to be taken to the underworld.

Soon you will meet Waskar, the Keeper of the Underworld. He will greet you. You will then be placed on the ground, where there will be many Guides to assist you. One of your Guides will open you up, take out your heart and place a brand new heart into your body. See all the Guides who are there to assist you by sending you healing light.

Be open to receiving a miraculous healing. The more you let go the easier and sooner it happens. Invite your new heart to live with you and have a new life. Forget about the old, leave the past behind here in the underworld. The Guides have taken your old heart and have given it to Mother Earth, where she will enlighten it and turn it into something good.

Your Guides will show you back up into your usual world, and more healing will take place. Surrender control and release all emotions here. When you feel the process is complete, come back to the bedrock, to the water, and bring back with you your power animal, to live with you and give you strength, courage, self-confidence and surety of a new you.

If you don't want to travel to the underworld, you can take the letter and burn it in a fire to release it to Spirit.

Angel Forgiveness Meditation:

You can do this meditation sitting, lying down or in yoga pose. Take a cleansing breath in and out, in and out, relax your entire body, and start noticing your breath. Breathe in and out; with every breath you take, you are getting more and more relaxed.

We call on you, Archangel Michael, Raphael, to come and assist me today with this healing. Shine your brilliant light on me and guide me.

Now visualize a beautiful white light underneath your feet. Allow this white light to travel up your body to your heart. Close your eyes and notice a beautiful red rose in front of you, at heart level. Allow the red rose to slowly open up until is it is completely open. Now visualize the name of the person you would like to forgive, and place his or her name in the center of the rose. (You can also do this with an animal's name). Place the name in the center of the rose and say: I am ready to release any anger, hatred or resentment I have toward you. Then state the name. I surrender, let go, and allow myself to release this. I love and forgive you, I love and forgive you, I love and forgive you - in all directions of time, at all levels, including the DNA level. Now see the rose slowly start to close, with the name inside, until it is all the way closed. Watch the rose slowly begin to disappear into thin air. The Angels have happily taken the rose with them as a gift. They are happy to help you. Say thank you, it is done, it is done, it is done. Amen.

Chapter Twelve
Healing in My Sleep

I know it might sound crazy, but it is possible to heal while you are sleeping. One day I was busy with so many clients, I hardly had time to take care of my own needs. I had told a friend that I would do healing work on her. She was counting on it, and I had every intention of making it happen. But before I knew it, the day was over and I had forgotten to do the healing.

I asked the Angels if it was at all possible to send her healing while I was sleeping. You will not believe what happened.

She was having problems walking. She had severe pain in her right leg, and even found it hard to get out of bed. She was not sure why she was experiencing this pain and discomfort. The Angels had me work on her while I was sleeping. I remember that in my dream they showed me sending healing light to her leg. I had done a reading while I was sleeping, and heard the Angels say that her situation had to do with feeling guilty and unworthy. Her problem was all about stepping into her own power; she was allowing other people to make decisions for her. Once Spirits removed all the guilt she was feeling and those who were affecting her energy field, they balanced all of her chakras and her body, I was then able to start on the healing process with the Spirits. As we all know, we are not the healers. It is totally the Divine that steps in and does its magic. I believe in magic and all that Spirits can do, they do not want us to be sick, it is clear; heal the mind, and your body and spirit will follow. When I got up the next morning, I remembered the dream vividly and told her everything that happened. She woke up feeling great, as if nothing bad had ever happened to her.

We are always putting limits on ourselves instead of asking for help and allowing Spirit to do everything for us. How comforting to know that we have Spirit's support and help at all times; all we have to do is ask. Since this incident, I have been asking the Angels to help me continue to heal while I am sleeping. So many people ask me for healing, but it is not possible due to time constraints. I would not ask someone to pay me; this is a favor that I do for friends and family.

The Angels have said that there are no limitations, and that all things are possible with God. We just have to make the conscious effort to remove all beliefs that are keeping us from seeing the truth; we are invincible and can do anything we put our heart and mind to.

Now, this next section may sound even crazier. The Angels have told me that anything you ask for right now as far as a healing, they will grant to you. The Angels will use my energy and all of my healing experience to initiate this.

You might ask yourself, how is that possible? Well, I have made an agreement, or should I say they have made an agreement and I have agreed, with God, my Spirit Guides and my Angels to use me whenever possible to heal someone who needs it.

I know that, just like the Angels, I can be omnipresent; I can be in more than one place at one time. I will never forget when they had me do healing work with an entire class all at once. I thought it was unreal, yet I knew how real it really was. They said; we will use you to make this happen.

Everyone in the class received a different kind of healing; some had a sense of wonder about why they felt so good. Others knew they had just let go of something huge in their life. One thing was for sure, not one person was the same when they left the class as when they came in.

One of my girlfriends keeps telling me I needed to be cloned. I knew this was a joke but sometimes I really felt like that was what I wanted and needed. Then I heard a voice saying, "You can do it all, we will use you to make it happen." Then, lo and behold, there it was, happening. One friend called me to tell me, "You were here with me while I was doing Feng Shui practice in my house. I felt your energy helping me." Another client told me, "I felt you this morning in my meditation. You were helping me remove blockages in my third eye." Still another friend remarked, "I asked that you come and help me with a situation I was having, and it worked. I could feel you healing me."

The stories are endless. This just goes to show that Spirits have no limitations.

I do not give myself credit for all that Spirit does. Instead, I praise Spirit every time I see what it does; it never ceases to amaze me.

Just as I can do this, I am sure you can as well. You do not have to have special favor with Spirit. We are all the same in the eyes of God. We all have favor with God; One love, one energy. We just have to change some of our belief systems and work on ourselves before we can attempt to do healing work on others. I truly believe we have to clean up our own river before we can enter into anyone else's river without polluting it.

So let's take this time to allow Spirit to work. I cannot guarantee anything, but I know that you will feel the healing take place, and that it will take you one step closer to where you want to go. Do not be surprised if Spirit does create a miracle. I believe in miracles and witness them almost every single day.

Say this prayer with me:

Dear God, Angels and Spirit Guides, I come to you humbly for a healing. May you heal me from (state your situation, even if more than one). I completely trust you and know it is being healed in all directions of time, and at all levels, especially on a DNA level, and for this I am grateful. I trust you and know that I deserve it. It is done, it is done, it is done, Thank You in advance. I love you! Amen.

Chapter Thirteen
God-Given Dream

We grow up with so many dreams of ourselves becoming so many different types of people. Then we realize that the dream was just a wish.

How do you know when what you experienced is a God-given dream? When it keeps haunting you and never really leaves you. You might say to yourself, but I cannot make a living doing what I love. However, since that is your God-given dream, God prepared you for it, gifted you with it, and planted the seed. All you have to do is nurture your dream to make it grow. You will be supported to make a living at what you love doing.

All too often, you put limitations on yourself or allow other people's limitations for you to limit you. You are directly influenced by their thoughts. Don't let *anyone* steal your joy.

Every day you make choices and when you realize that you are infinite, omnipresent, and limitless; then your choices will change.

You know that you *need* to do something, instead of that you *should* do something, so the outcome will change.

I have seen situations where God tries to give someone a message, but they will not listen. I remember when a dear friend of mine was in a car accident that left her bedridden for over six months. She loved to write but always gave herself an excuse as to why she could not do it. She would mention her family, her friends her job, anything she could think of to stop writing. Although she did not like her job, she felt stuck because she had to pay the bills. But she used to say to me all the time, "I would love to write a book one day," and look up at the clouds and start day-dreaming about all the great things she wanted to write about. I told her just do it, but she would laugh and brush off my advice. "Yes, one day," she would say.

Well, that one day was forced on her when she was bedridden. She told me she heard a voice that said, "Do you finally get it? Start writing!" She was blown away, started writing, and finished her book in less than five months. She said, "What a shame that it took that wakeup call, but I'm so grateful, and now I look at the blessing."

We do not need something drastic to happen in order to wake up. We all have free will. But wouldn't it be nice to just change the way we think so that we get out of our own way and allow God to do what He does best, fulfill our every dream?

You can manifest what you want faster by just knowing, acting, breathing, feeling that it is a must, that there are no choices between yes or no, there is only yes. You choose to, you need to fulfill this choice. When you choose to do something, you are making a decision in the moment about your emotional, spiritual, and physical state, about how you will respond to your life situation.

When I was growing up, I had so many aspirations and dreams. My sister Angela used to say to me, "You change your career every time you go to the bathroom." I have had so many jobs! I have been a make-up artist, an appraiser, a dental hygienist, a saleswoman, a mortgage broker, and a realtor. My biggest move was when I changed from working in the corporate world to the spiritual world. I can honestly say now I am living one of my dearest dreams.

I grew up believing we need to put food on the table, so we have to get a long-lasting job that pays well. But I was never really good at working for anyone else. I had my own make-up line when I was 18, and after that, I was the owner of a mortgage and real estate company for over 12 years. I never thought I could make a living doing what I really loved to do.

Teaching, writing and doing healing work are my strongest passions. But I never would have arrived at this point if I had not changed my belief system! If we believe the Universe will supply us with the things we love to do, then the Universe has no other choice than to honor that belief so search deep into your soul and ask yourself, if it wasn't for the money, what would I be doing right now? See yourself doing it. How does that feel in your heart, in your gut? If it feels right to you, thank the Creator ahead of time, as if the situation is already here. You will be surprised as to how soon it will arrive, and how much money you will get as well.

But if we make money our main focus for success, we soon come to realize that if the money does come easily, it also goes easily.

When we make service and love our life purpose and criteria for success, our goals are long-lasting and healthy.

Chapter Fourteen
Hidden Greatness

You may have a hidden greatness inside of you. I believe we all do; we just have to open up to the possibility y. We are all born with greatness, but most of the time it is hidden. We often get too comfortable in life, not wanting to make any changes or sacrifices, or even open up to other possibilities. If we get busy having fun, doing what we love to do, we will find a hidden greatness. Never stop finding yourself.

We do not need a crisis to uncover a hidden greatness. Anthony Burgess was told he only had a short time to live because he had cancer. When he was given that news, he started writing non-stop. Before he knew it, he had written 70 books and to his amazement, all of his cancer disappeared.

We can challenge ourselves without having to face tragedy or illness. How would you live differently? What exactly would you do if you wanted to challenge yourself?

Creating small changes that become permanent; big changes often create frustration. We give up. If you want to be a writer and have writer's block, just write something, even if it's badly written. This is also called self-motivation. Almost all good writers begin with terrible efforts, says Anne Lamott in her book "Shitty First Drafts." The key to writing is to just start. Write anything. It can be the worst piece you have ever written; that doesn't matter.

When you are in the first stage of creating, do not censor yourself. The mere fact of doing takes you out of the "What if" stage, takes you out of making excuses and the pessimistic thought process. So just start writing. You will be pleasantly surprised at what will come next.

Are you a singer? An artist? An athlete? Do you love to play with children? If you are not sure of your talents or believe that you have some hidden greatness inside of you wanting to get out, ask your Angels and Guides to help you. Archangel Gabriel is especially good for bringing out your best talents.

You can create your own prayer or use this one.

Talent Prayer: *Archangel Gabriel, I come to you now. Please guide me to my hidden greatness. What is it that I am good at doing that I am not aware of? What additional talents are hidden in me that you would like to disclose? I am open to hearing your messages. I completely trust you and know you are guiding me.*

Please help me release any fears I have of showing my talents, and any fears I have of success. I completely surrender to a Higher Source and know that all of my talents will be revealed to me. I am forever grateful. Thank you. Amen

Chapter Fifteen
Control Thoughts

Do you ever have a conversation with someone and know what they are thinking? They are not talking, but you can practically hear them screaming in your ear.

We are all made up of thoughts; our life is thoughts. We have in our life today a reflection of our thoughts yesterday, today and what we will be thinking tomorrow. What if there was a way to control our thoughts, to avoid thinking of things we did not want to think about? What if we could have the power to change our thoughts? Well, the good news is we do have that power; we just have to put it into practice. We have to decide to make a conscious effort to change our thoughts. In return, our world will reflect what we are thinking.

We can create any thoughts that we like. But we must understand the process of thought creation. The thought comes with intent, whenever we like and under any circumstance. Let's take a second to analyze the process of thinking. There are three factors to consider: First, the pattern. This is the deepest impression, as it goes predominantly to ideas and the clearest image. Second, is mental substance, whose quality improves with the quality of the mind. When our consciousness is expanded, the quality of the mind increases. Third, the creative energies grow stronger when we awaken the greater power from within. As we start to impress our minds with our own ideas, regardless of what is going on around us, we place our destiny in our own hands.

Recognizing that thoughts are real, the external world is a reflection, a mirror of our internal world. We are composed of thought, mental states and mental activities. When our thoughts change, we change. Our thoughts are patterns of the pictures we have placed in our minds. Paint the picture well. Create the vision you want. Once you have created it, continue it for a sufficient length of time to give the creative process, the opportunity to make the change in your whole self.

"The more I learn, the more I can help myself and others." My learning capacity is infinite.

When I place a certain picture in my mind, my thoughts will create the likelihood of it coming to pass. But as a rule, it takes time to change the entire self. Therefore, I must continue to hold the desired picture in mind until the whole self has become just like the picture and I have created the change, the shift.

When the new self has made the change and the negative has changed to the positive, we will attract new things.

It is possible to attract the new and the old if we only Change one of our thoughts and not the others.

Thought is a power source. It is magnetic and manifests things into reality. We are constantly vibrating at a current frequency that starts in our thought process, in our minds. Just like headlights or electricity has frequency, so do we. Oftentimes, we can feel the thought vibrations of others. Our thoughts are affecting us and influencing others all the time. People do not have to say a word, and yet we can be affected by how someone else is thinking. It is up to us how we want to respond. It has now become our decision. Thoughts of love will attract more thoughts of love. Thoughts of gossip will attract more gossip into your life. So guard your thoughts wisely.

If you find yourself in a situation that feels like gossip, get out of it quickly, as it will only bring more gossip into your life. Gossip is like poison, slowly eating you up. I believe gossip is very ugly and keeps us away from our blessings. We have to remain clear and clean of this. Oftentimes, you might find yourself manifesting new friends; the old must be washed away in order for new things to come into your life.

I have never had a problem letting go of friends who did not serve me. However, I only had to do this once. I was aware of the effect someone was having on me. I know we are all mirrors of each other, so I choose to see a mirror of what I want to see and be, not of what I do not want.

Thoughts of defeat or of being a victim are also thoughts that can destroy us. Once we claim responsibility for ourselves and stop blaming other people, circumstances, God or the world for our lives, then we can get out of our way and start creating our thoughts instead of allowing negative thoughts to control us.

Chapter Sixteen

The Magnificent Brain

We all have a magnificent brain. Learning how to use it is the key to happiness.

In 1950, Roger W. Sperry of the University of Chicago (later of Cal Tech) made a great discovery – that dreams, energy and creative insight come from the right side of the brain, while logical, short-term, linear and short-sighted thinking come from the left side of the brain.

If we were to use our right brains more often, we would be in a happier state of mind, because we would be in a purpose state.   When we have a purpose, we have a direction, a desire to fulfill. But if we spent most of the day on the logical left side of the brain, we are simply letting life live us, instead of us living life. The right side of the brain is more in line with who we really are.   Our higher self is expressed at this state of being. Meditating, daydreaming and manifesting are the role of the right brain.

The left brain tells the right side what to do. "Do not die with the music still inside you."

While the right brain comes alive at night, the left brain sleeps. We can activate both sides of the brain; we simply have to fire up the left brain to call on the right brain.

How good does it feel to hold a baby, play games,

write poetry, sing, dance or be silly?   The left brain commands the right side to come alive and get involved. That is what psychologist Abraham Maslow called "peak experiences."

Your dreams are magical. You can bring your dreams into wake time. Your life can become magical!

You are a magnetic magical being, so allow the magic inside you to come alive. You are the creator, the director of your own life. Making time to play, to visualize your desired life and to incorporate joy in your life will bring you to that magical place. This is how you align both sides of the brain.

Remember how fascinating the story of Cinderella was? She would daydream all the time about being with her prince, until one day her dream came true.

It does not matter. The brain cannot differentiate between daydreaming and night dreaming, as everything is energy. Daydream enough until that dream comes true.

Know that your thoughts and actions are magnetic.

If you hold a thought long enough, it begins to come alive. It begins to develop your experiences and to become a part of you. It becomes you! I have heard it said, "Be careful what you wish for, it may come true. I also like to say, "Be careful what you think of, because it will become you."

All of our fears are self-created. If we have the ability to create it, we have the ability to confront it. As tempting as it is to ignore fear and live in the safe zone; we will not be happy until we confront our fears and transform them into power. Our fears are real. Sometimes we have no idea where they came from, whether from a past life, an ancestral tie, life experiences, or if we were just born with them. But one thing we know for sure is that they are real.

The best way to face them is to acknowledge that they exist. It is easy to ignore realities in life until they become too big.

Write down now the things you fear the most. Know that these things are becoming a part of your blueprint. Removing them would be a clear sign that you will not experience them in your life. Confront them and turn that energy into power.

This Meditation will help you.

Removing Fear Meditation:

Visualize white cords going down your ankles; allow these cords to travel down, sending them to the bottom of your feet. Go down, all the way down to Mother Earth. She ignites her brilliant energy and sends bright white light right back up, traveling up your feet, your ankles, your legs, your thighs. Allow this white light to travel to your root chakra, the base of your spine. Allow the white light to spin clockwise to cleanse and open up the root chakra, traveling up to your sacral chakra (three inches below your belly button), cleansing and opening your sacral chakra, keep going up to your solar plexus (the center of your stomach), cleaning and opening your solar plexus. Keep going up to your heart center, cleaning and opening your heart chakra, traveling up to your throat, cleaning in a clockwise motion and opening up your throat chakra, going up, cleansing and opening up your third eye (in between your eyebrows). Keep going up to your crown (the top of your head), cleansing and opening the crown.

Now visualize a gold pyramid on top of your head. See yourself going inside the pyramid; you are at the bottom of the pyramid, lying down, sitting or standing, whatever feels most comfortable to you. God is above you and your fear is above God. See what your fear is. Now send white light to God; see God send the white light to your fear. See what your fear is.

Now visualize this pyramid entering through the top of your head, coming down, down your third eye, down your throat, down through your heart. Now send a red cord to God. See God send the red cord to your fear. Your fear sends the red cord back to God. God turns this red into pink with his bright light, turning it into love. He sends you a beautiful pink cord. You send it back to Him and you look upward. Your fear has disappeared.

Prayer for Removing Fear:

Angels Divine, please down ray beautiful pink light down my energy centers. Remove all fear that is binding me at this time. I trust and know it is already done. I thank you in advance. Thank you. It is done, it is done, it is done. Amen.

With God, all things are possible. Know that you can do anything and everything through God who gives you strength. (Ephilpans 4:13)

Chapter Seventeen

Angels Among Us

We all have Angels among us and they are here to help and guide us. We also have specific angels for specific situations; embarking on these Angels can help your life become more fulfilling. Select the angels of your choice or simply just call on your guardian Angels. Most people think of financial gain when it comes to identifying abundance. However, abundance can also be an abundance of health, well-being, joy, and care free life style, free from stress, more peace, a fulfilling relationship, steady job, hobbies, love of family and friends and so much more. Inviting your Angels into your life is rewarding and sometimes often forgotten. Our Angels want to help and are so happy when we ask for assistance. Below we will identify some Angels.

Angel of Abundance: Angel Tyler, he maximizes the flow and accelerates prosperity by supplying the fuel and resources for happiness and financial security. Angel Tyler wants to help you experience abundance in your life; he knows all things are possible when you have abundance in your life. Call on Angel Tyler when you want to create good fortune, when you want to raise funds quickly, or when you want to enhance your resources. Prayers: You can use the prayers provided or you can use your own.

Prayer: *Angel Tyler, I come to you now to help me to have more Abundance in my life. I affirm that I generate true abundance and that I have all the resources I need for abundance. Thank you. Amen.*

Angel of Opportunity: Angel Christopher, he helps you be at the right place at the right time. He has the wisdom and the knowledge to know this. He will help you open doors and help you to walk through them. He is sharp and fast he will assist and give you knowledge to identity an opportunity when it arises. He will assist you with your talents and abilities; he will help you with your personal and professional life. Keep this angel by your side often.

Prayer: *Angel Christopher, I come to you now to help me with more opportunities, help me to make positive changes in my life, help to open doors, even the ones that seem shut, help me to advance to my true path to success. I affirm that all opportunities come to me now. I am open to new opportunities, and I am prosperous and successful always. Thank you. Amen.*

Angel of Manifestation: Angel Evelyn, she is the Angel to call on when you would like your dreams to come true. She will assist you and give you encouragement. She will help you to increase your ability to manifest your deepest desire. She is the Angel of wealth, success and abundance. Call on her when you are getting ready to enter a new chapter in your life. Call on her when manifesting prosperity is a priority; she will assist you in attracting all aspects having to do with manifestation.

Prayer: *Angel Evelyn, I call on you now. Help me to manifest my dreams to come true, I am a manifesting magnet, I have the lifestyle that I desire, all manifestations are open for me I humbly accept them. Thank you. Amen.*

Angel of Employment: Angel Philip will assist you in finding Employment; he will help you find a suitable position. He will assist you with the confidence and help to match your unique skills. He promotes favorable work situations and helps you sustain successful careers. Call on Angel Philip when you are entering the work force for the first time, when you want a better position or when you want to improve your current work status.

Prayer: *Angel Philip, I call on you now. Help me with my Employment needs. I affirm that I am successful in my position and all of my Employment needs and desires are being taken care of. I have the confidence and encouragement that I need to move forward. Thank you. Amen.*

Angel of Financial Security: Angel Jeremiah, will help you gain multiple income streams. He is especially talented to assist you with a solid foundation of wealth. He will help you sprout financial growth while supporting your path to prosperity. He will assist you with a more affluent life style. Call on Angel Jeremiah with any financial solutions you might need.

Prayer: *Angel Jeremiah, I come to you now for assistance in my financial security. May I always have financial security and may I make wise future investment. I affirm that I have financial security and always have a stream of income coming in at all times. Thank you. Amen.*

Angel of Protection: Archangel Michael is the Angel of protection. His name means "He who is like God." He is the Angel of righteousness and repentance. He is the most well-known Archangel who strengthens our spirit during difficult times or if you are in a dangerous situations. Archangel Michael inspires truth, love and patience. He is the patron Angel of policemen who guards and guides them as they work to protect us. He is also the Angel who leads our soul to heaven. He is one of my favorite Angels. Establishing a close relationship with Archangel Michael can change your life. Keep him by your side often.

Prayer: *Archangel Michael, come to me now. Guard and protect me always. Keep me in my truth, patience and love. If I feel troubled or afraid or feel like the world is closing in on me, come and fight for me, protect me. I affirm that my life is easy and effortless because of you. Thank you. Amen.*

Angel of Healing: Archangel Raphael, his name means "Divine Healer" he is a well-known Angel who is known for extreme healing energy, which he bestows on everyone. Call on him if you are sick or doing healing work, or are praying for someone who is sick or just needs healing for any reason. He also has the ability to grant us many things, including joy, grace and love. He encourages us to be self-motivated so we can become who we desire to be.

Prayer: *Archangel Raphael, come to me now, send your healing energy to me. I affirm that I am a Divine manifestation of God's goodness. I desire more for myself; a healthier body, a joyful heart, a happier home, and a loving state of mind. May everyone who comes to me feel your healing energy. Empower my hands with your light, my heart with your love that I may live in your healing energy always. Thank you. Amen.*

Angel of Messenger: Archangel Gabriel, his name means "Strength in God." Gabriel carries and instills Love, Truth, joy, justice and grants wisdom in interpreting dreams and visions. He is especially helpful in times of premonitions and clairvoyance. This Angel's purpose is to do the will of God. Archangel Gabriel is a teacher and a messenger of Truth.

Prayer: *Archangel Gabriel Come to me now and in my dreams that I may be able to interpret my dreams. I am open to the messages that come to me. I affirm that I hear the messages from God loud and clear. I am ready to receive the messages right now. Thank you. Amen.*

Angel of Creative Power: Archangel Jophiel, is the Angel of

beauty, letting you see the beauty in everything, and helps you attract and manifest more beauty in your life. He is the Archangel Angel of illumination, wisdom, laughter and light. He will help you pass tests and exams. He will help you be more creative and assist you in all of your creative powers, in your relationships and your career.

Prayer: *Archangel Jophiel, come to me now. I am ready to open up my creative powers I am ready to see the beauty in everyone and in everything. I affirm that I am very creative and I am ready to explore this creativity even more. I know that I create what I think. Help me to think of only those things that will expand my creativity. Thank you. Amen.*

Angel of Prayer and Compassion: Archangel Zadkiel, he radiates comfort to those who are grieving, wounded or afraid. He is the Angel of charity, comfort and gentleness. He assists us in helping us find compassion, and helping us forgive others to free ourselves. He is the Archangel who guards the powers and requests and also simulates spiritual development.

Prayer: *Archangel Zadkiel, come to me now. Assist me in all areas of my life that need to be looked at and improve. If I am holding on to un-forgiveness, please help me to release it. Help all my prayers to be delivered to God. Help me to focus on the correct prayers for myself and others. I affirm that all of my prayers are being answered and heard. My prayerful heart easily connects me to God. Thank you. Amen.*

Angel of Tolerance, Adoration and Love: Archangel Chamuel, his name means "He who sees God." He inspires us to realize that we must first love ourselves. Archangel Chamuel will help you dissolve feelings of selfishness, self- condemnation and low self-esteem. He is especially helpful with relationships, helping mend and repair damaged relationships. He will assist you in getting along with others. He will also assist in finding new friends and healthy relationships. Archangel Chamuel specializes in charity, love, compassion, mercy, creativity and forgiveness. He is also very talented in helping you find lost objects and finding a job or finding a great parking space. This is a great Angel to have by your side.

Prayer: *Archangel Chamuel, come to me now. Help me to understand how important it is to love myself first, to pull any feeling of selfishness or any negative energy I might be holding for myself or anyone else. Help me to view my own short comings. I affirm that all of my relationships are healthy. I am attracting love and true intimacy with my perfect partner. Thank you. Amen.*

These are just a few of the Angel that may guide you along the way to enhance your experiences in life, I encourage you to connect with them often or find other Angels of your choice. I have always had a very close relationship with my Angels and I do not know what I would do without them. However I understand if we do not know of

their blessings we could be shutting ourselves from one of
the most precious gifts of life.

Chapter Eighteen
Finding Yourself

I write this chapter with anticipation that someone will read this and recognize if they are living the life God wants for them. I would like to share a story of a situation in my life where the person I cared for the most decided to disconnect from me. She is the most precious and dear person to me in the whole wide world my sister Angela, I feel she is my other half; as if though we were twins in another life time. If she feels something I feel it and vice versa. It was over fifteen year ago that this incident happened but the angels wanted me to bring it up, so you can recognize the signs when something is inappropriate and when someone is in an occult.

My sister Angela has always been so sweet she is just like an angel. She never saw the bad or evil in anyone. She walked around trusting everyone as if though she had blind folds on. She never understood why anyone would do a person any harm. From the outside you would look at her and think she lived a normal life; she had a husband, a great job, she was extremely bright and beautiful. She was searching to fill a void inside of her or searching for truth of some kind, something that would fulfill her heart. She wanted to have a closer relationship with God. Since we were brought up quite religious, she felt like her soul was reaching out for a deeper connection.

She had a friend at work that noticed her interest in God. She was very well-versed in the bible and it seemed to be the perfect match. Well Angela had no idea what she was getting herself into; it seemed innocent enough.

Let's call this friend Diane. Diane was very outgoing and knew everyone at the church she attended. She was smart and knew just the right words to say.

One day I asked Angela to introduce me to her friend Diane; I wondered why Angela never had the time to hang out with me anymore. I was starting to get a bit suspicious.

Angela had no problem with that and was very excited that I would be meeting her trusted friend. One of the biggest gifts I've been given is being able to tell who is who. I can see someone and tell you all about them; I do not even need to shake their hand. I met Diane and it took everything I had not to throw up on her. I got sick to my stomach when I saw her. I knew she was bad news. I did not know how to let Angela down and let her know that Diane was not the person she was portraying to be.

I tried to talk to Angela and tell her a few things I did not like that Diane did, but Angela just blew it off. I asked Diane to invite me to the Church she was taking my sister to; she hesitated at first but then finally said yes. I wanted to check out the church that Angela and Diane loved so much. I agreed to meet Angela and Diane at their work place and follow them from there; I lived further away so it made more since to take my own car.

We started to drive off. I was following Diane very easily, and then all of the sudden, out of nowhere, Diane tries to lose me on the expressway. She started going so fast and changing lanes as if though she was in some professional race car competition. I knew this was a clear sign that she was trying to lose me. We did not have cell phones at the time only beepers and this would not help me find the location. I did not have the address or the name of the church, but I was determined to keep up with her to make sure I would make it there. I know the Angels where helping me get there in one piece. They were opening the way in every direction that I wanted. As I was passing lane to lane, I prayed to my Angels and God to help me. I think I was praying the entire half an hour non-stop until I arrived.

When I arrived at the church and got out of the car, I looked at Diane. I thought I was looking at the Devil herself. She was so angry that I had made it without a sweat. She knew she would not have the same impact on Angela if I was there.

Apparently, she was trying to get Angela to believe that the church wanted her to leave her family to follow Jesus. She had already brainwashed her to believe; if you are not equally yoked, then you must sacrifice your life for God and leave your family behind.

She had an alternative motive and it was to take

money from her. She would tell Angela that since she prayed for her she had to pay her and start supporting her. She told Angela that she was the church and that God did everything she wanted. She had Angela so convinced and scared that she did everything Diane asked her to do. Angela saw Diane do witchcraft on her husband so he would lose his job. When it happened, Angela was very upset but could not do anything about it.

Angela started to talk like Diane and was taken over by her energy; she was just like her. She excluded herself from the family and lost her husband.

I prayed for her every day. Every time I wanted to talk to her, she would hang up the phone and say, "I am sorry I cannot talk to you." Her spirit was already gone; she was carrying around Diane's spirit. The Angela I knew and grew up with was hiding somewhere deep down inside, I knew she was there.

I cried myself to sleep many nights just asking God to bring her back. I felt like a part of me had died because she was like my twin. One only needs to be a twin to understand the strong connection you have with your twin, I don't think there are words in the dictionary to describe its depth.

Two years went by and Angela had disappeared from the family. One day she had to come by my parents" house for something and I happened to be there. I could not keep still. I was asking the Angels to help me to open her eyes; I asked them to illuminate her to see the truth.

I went to the room where she was, looked straight into her eyes and said, "Angela I love you, but please Come back, Come back!" I screamed out loud, "Can't you see you are brainwashed." Mom and the whole family are so upset. "Open your eyes," I screamed, "Open your eyes!" I had lots of tears coming down my face. "This is not you," I yelled out to her, "Come back! Come back!" She looked at me and I knew I had gotten to her. She started crying and said, "I am so sorry I was so scared and brainwashed, I see that now. How did I let this happen to me, she took everything from me, my furniture, all of my money, everything. She took everything from me," she kept saying... I told her it would be alright and the most important thing was that she gets her soul back. That she comes back to the person she was meant to be, that she comes back to herself again. She realized at that moment that she had actually lost her identify and didn't even know who she was anymore.

The beautiful child God made her to be, full of love and joy; she had not smiled for over two years. It was all pain and tears for her. Wow, how could someone live this way? I told her, you do not deserve this, you deserve to be happy. She hugged me and said you are right. I will never speak to her again. I knew the Angels had their hands on this and I was so appreciative of this miracle that just took place. The Angels stepped in to save the day. I knew the timing was right because I was determined to say my peace right then and there.

She must have cried for days feeling so bad about how she hurt Mom, me and the family. But all was forgiven and forgotten. She had to find herself again by re-connecting with old friends and family. But most importantly she did a "Soul Retrieval" to bring her back to who she was always meant to be. She instantly stepped back into her power and has since been the most remarkable sister anyone could ever have. She was later blessed with a wonderful new husband and a beautiful child.

The Angels want you to notice if you are being directed to leave your family. God wants the family to love each other and be together, do not let any religion or someone else's belief system fool you into believing anything different.

A family is a blessing, and this is the family you chose before you were born, just like you chose your Parents. Be thankful for your family, they are your family. However do not let anyone treat you disrespectfully; you deserve to be respected no matter who it is.

Don't let anyone influence you to be someone you are not. Step into your power and in all circumstances ask God is this what you want for me. Guide me at all times and show me the truth.

Here is a poem I wrote when this happened in my life.

"I am Here"

I know you've often wondered where I've been if I can hear you, feel you or if I have been your friend.

I know you've often wondered where to go or where to turn. The times you did not know which way you would get burned.

But somehow I directed you, I showed you some kind of sign, when you looked up to me, I was right there by your side.

I know you've often wondered why time stands still and nothing seems to flow, why troubles come and do not seem to go.

I know you've often wondered why things seem so unfair, but no matter what you go through, I am always there.

I know you've often wondered why you should even call my name, would it make a difference or would it be the same.

I know you've often wondered what faith would do for you, if it would change the things you say or do.

I know you've often wondered why you should give your life to me; maybe too many changes would become of thee.

Well, I've come to take away your confusion; I've come to take away your fear. I am God who loves you and who holds your every tear!

Elsa Ramirez copyright© 1995

Chapter Nineteen
Soul Retrieval

Have you ever felt lost or felt like you are not yourself? Have you felt rejected or abandoned by God and others? Have you felt powerless or done things to self-sabotage yourself? Have you felt shame, isolated, had difficulty in relationships, fear of intimacy, co-dependent? Or perhaps you're an overachiever or a perfectionist. These are just a few of the feelings you might experience when you are in need of a soul retrieval.

Have you had surgery, a divorce, lost a loved one or served in the military? The Shamans believe we can lose our spiritual energy because of such events; when this happens, it is called a soul loss. When a piece of our soul's energy splits from us, it returns to Mother Earth where it feels safe, until a shaman retrieves that soul piece and gives it back to us.

A soul loss can happen either through an emotional or physical trauma. When you experience trauma, part of your energy can get stuck in that time and place. Your body will go into survival mechanism because it might be more than your body can handle, to experience the full trauma.

In the Inca tradition, the belief is that as you continue to evolve, deeper layers of your soul loss may be revealed to you, and so you will probably need more than one soul retrieval session.

The Shaman's role is to retrieve the soul piece that is gone and help bring you back into your power. A shamanic healing is a spiritual method that deals with healing from a spiritual aspect. It is believed that spiritual blockages can cause illness in a localized area of your body. The Shaman knows just where to extract and remove these harmful energies from a body.

I have had the pleasure of assisting countless of soul retrievals. I would have to say that the most rewarding aspect of being a Shaman is the blessing you receive when the session is over. When you see the smile on the client's face, when you see that he or she has completely changed and you know that a miracle just took place, you feel exceptionally rewarded to have been a part of that sacred journey. Sometimes when you are a Shaman, you will see that although the client is in need of a soul retrieval, he or she is not ready for it yet. That means there are other healings that need to take place before the body can fully integrate a soul retrieval.

The Medicine people of the Andes believe we can continue to grow spiritually throughout our lives. It is up to us how we choose to live our life. We can create a new world for ourselves; we just have to appreciate all the resources that are available to us.

When a Shaman is doing a soul retrieval, he or she

will retrieve three pieces for the client; a medicine gift, a soul element and a power animal.

I would like to tell you of a soul retrieval that stays very close to my heart. My brother Mario was in the hospital battling cancer. I was out of town at the time and so could not attend to him in person. I had told him I would do a healing for him as soon as I returned, but he was not in any position to talk to me then. However, one day as I woke up I heard his voice loud and clear, saying, "Help me, please help me." His Higher Self was asking me to help him. I did not go to class that morning, since I had no doubt what I was supposed to do.

I got on my knees and prayed, "God, help me to do Your will. Let me know what You want me to do for Mario. Save him, God, save him." I did not want to lose my brother; the thought was way too painful, so I stayed hopeful and obedient.

Then I heard a voice saying, "Do a soul retrieval!"

I was very eager to get started, and traveled into the underworld to meet Waskar, the Keeper of the Underworld. He showed me that Mario had drawn up a contract saying that he did not deserve to live; it was a form of punishment for whatever he felt guilty about from other lifetimes. I asked Waskar if we could change the contract and he said yes. Mario's new contract says that he deserves to live and that he wants to live.

We came back from the underworld with Mario's soul

piece, a medicine gift (a beautiful green stone), and a power animal (a black panther).

Upon my arrival back in Florida, I was anxious to see my brother Mario. I got to the hospital and noticed that he looked different, happier, and more content. I gave him the beautiful green stone, and he instantly clasped it in his hand and was fascinated by it. He started to rub it all over his body and said, "I want to live, I want to live!" I could not believe my eyes, this is exactly what Waskar and I had just been working on. My brother smiled at me and said, "I love this stone!" He was quite sedated because of the pain medication but, considering all that he had been through, he looked good.

I told him that I had just done a healing on him, and he said he knew that because he felt it. He was just beginning to open up to the idea that there are other ways to heal besides working with doctors and therapists. He held my hand tightly and indicated that everything would be all right. Mario had fully stepped into his power. He said he had surrendered to the will of God.

My brother lasted for three more months, but could not hold on any longer. The doctors could not understand how he was holding on as long as he did because the cancer had spread so widely through his body. I was sure it was because of his new contract. I know that when he comes back, he will die of old age, as a very healthy person. The healing he cried out for did not go unnoticed; he was able to be with us longer and as I say, I know will last into eternity.

The healing you do today lasts forever, and affects everyone around you.

Chapter Twenty
True Love

What is true love? I would have to say true love is when we are focused on energy that we know makes us feel, act and be complete, whether it is love of ourselves or of someone else. If we wish to manifest a certain thing in our life, we must love the very thing we wish to obtain and continue loving it.

If we allow this strong intent to be sidetracked, we will lose the very thing we wish to manifest. Nothing but intense love will enable you to surmount the many obstacles placed in your path.

Love and desire go hand in hand. The more desire we have for a thing, the more we love it; and the more we love it, the greater will the attractive force be exerted toward its attainment, both within ourselves and outside of ourselves.

There is nothing stronger than love. Oftentimes I have been asked, what is the meaning of life. The very first thing I say is Love.

What can we do today to love ourselves more? What changes could we create to manifest more of what we love? Did you know if we are messy and do not take care of our home or our car this is a direct reflection of the love we are not feeling toward our self? So look around you. Are you loving yourself enough to do what is best for you? Are you addressing the very thing you are trying to ignore? Get rid of the clutter or it will overpower your energy. It will have you feeling sick and blue. It is like a stop sign to all of your manifestations. Organize your life, your space. I know the more we live in the right side of the brain, it becomes a lot harder to be organized, because this is a left brain function. Ask your Angels to help you with this. All it takes is a simple prayer and the Angels are on it instantly. They will give you a peace about it and have you tackle one thing at a time. Do not try to do it all in one day; small steps create the big changes.

Also ask your Angels to help you to love yourself more, to allow more play time and fun in your life. Ask them to help you receive, if you have any issues about receiving. Did your parents allow you to have fun while you were growing up? If not, this could affect you in your adult years and even carry over to your own children. So, the sooner you open yourself up to this realization, the better. Ask the Angels to help you break through it. You do not need to have permission from your parents to have fun.

In the Shamanic tradition, you are guided to bring your soul piece back with you so you can be the person you have always been meant to be. If life gets too serious or if you experienced a trauma in life, sometimes this soul piece leaves. I have had to do a soul retrieval, and it really made a difference in my life. Most of the clients Spirits bring to me need a soul retrieval. Like attracts like, so if you have been through something in your life, you will attract the same energies in your life to help in some way.

A soul retrieval will bring back that soul piece that left when it did not feel safe. You might have to experience other healings before you get to this one. Your Spirit knows when you are ready, but in the meantime, ask your Angels to show you if this is a healing you need. Your Angels are very powerful and will keep you in a good place, so be open to their messages at all times.

Chapter Twenty-One
Healing from the Departed

Can you imagine, just for a second, receiving a healing from a deceased loved one, or having to give a healing to someone who has already crossed over? In this chapter I will tell you of occurrences that I have seen or experienced hands-on, that left me feeling such a sense of comfort, knowing it is never too late to heal.

The first story I will tell you happened to my sister Angela. She was at work one day and started to feel an immense pain in her left arm. It was getting so uncomfortable; she found it hard to move her arm at all. It started to progressively get worse and her arm seemed to turn into what felt like jelly. She called me from work in a panic. "Elsa, I do not know what is going on with my left arm. I am getting concerned. It hurts like crazy and has gotten to the point where I cannot control the muscles; it feels like jelly." I asked the Angels to show me what was going on. A voice said, "She needs a healing. Her body is spent, and she needs to come and see you."

Angela said she was going to go to a clinic to check the arm out, but I told her, "You are wasting your time," yet I understood. She went to the clinic and the doctor told her he had never seen this before. He recommended that she get an M.R.I. done right away. She called me to ask what I thought. I told her, "You have two choices here: get the M.R.I and they will not find anything wrong with you, or come here and get a healing." She asked, what about the pain? I said, "What about it?" I think she had forgotten how powerful Spirits are, and all that they can do. She agreed with me and said, "I trust you. I am on my way."

She arrived, and we got right to work. I started channeling to receive messages as to what would be best for her. Suddenly my Dad came through and said, "I want to help. Will you let me enter your body?" This is known as a Physical Medium. Physical Mediumship is the process whereby someone, in Spirit, usually known as a spirit operator (as compared to a spirit communicator), works or operates through the mental AND physical energies of the Medium and causes something physical to happen on the Earth plane. Physical Mediumship is objective in nature; that is, when the phenomena occur, everyone is able to see and/or hear them.

I was very happy to let my Dad work on my sister; after all, she is his daughter, and he wanted to help. My Dad was a natural healer in his own right. When he was alive, he would put his hands on someone and instantly send healing that would usually lead to a miraculous healing. He said that he would ask Jesus to come through his hands, and he could feel heat coming out of them. It is quite spectacular to watch.

So, Dad was ready to get to work on Angela. She laid down and Dad started to put his hands over her. I could feel the heat coming out of my hands; naturally, since it was not my hands at all, it was really Dad's hands. Dad started speaking to Angela, "What are you doing to yourself? Stop feeling so guilty. It is not your fault; you did all you could do." He was referring to my Mom, when my brother Mario died. On the way to the funeral, my Mom fell down and broke her kneecap in three places. She managed to make it to the funeral, but then had to be rushed to the emergency room right after that. Angela had been feeling guilty that she was not there for Mom and all that she went through, first losing her son and then having this terrible accident.

Angela had a new son, so she had to make sure she was attending to her home life. My Dad hugged Angela and said, "Please let this guilt go, because you deserve to be happy. I am very proud of you. Please forgive me; I never really hugged you enough." Angela started crying like she had never cried before and put her left arm around Dad, hugged him and forgot all about the pain. The pain had gone away, and the muscles in her arm came back to normal.

The next story has to do with a client that came in to see me. Starr had her deceased loved one around all the time. She told me, "Elsa, my Dad does not want to leave me. He does not want to go to the light. I have gone to other healers and tried everything, but nothing is working. Can you please help?" I said, "Sure." She knew her Dad was around because he would talk to her and give her signs all the time. She said it was making her a bit upset. We scheduled a day for the healing. She arrived at my doorstep and said, "My Dad will not let me go inside, he knows I want him to leave." I said,

"That's fine, just come in and let's talk. Let's just start there." She hesitated, and then finally said, "Okay, fine, let's talk.

She came inside. Not two minutes into the conversation, I felt a rush come over my body. I saw that her Dad was standing next to her. I told her, "Your Dad, is here and wants to talk." She said great. "Hi, Dad, how are you? Can you tell me why you will not go to the light?" He said, "Because I feel I have to be forgiven." She said, "Oh, Dad, of course you are forgiven. I forgive you for anything you ever did wrong." He said, "No, I have to forgive myself and I cannot do it." Part of the healing work I do is what I call Angel DNA reprogramming, changing energy from a negative to a positive on a DNA level.

I knew he wanted me to help, so I asked him to give me permission to change his belief system of "I forgive myself, no" to "I love and forgive myself." He said, "Yes, you have my permission." I asked the Angels to come in and help, and it was done almost instantly. The Angels started doing healing on him, sending him beautiful gold light. He was ready to go to the light now. Before he left, he showed me his throat with lots of cigarettes coming out of it and lots of smoke. I told Starr what he was showing me and she said,

"Yes, he used to smoke like a chimney." I saw that this is what killed him. She confirmed that he died of throat cancer.

He gave me other messages to give to Starr, and I saw his friend Jackie was there ready to receive him, along with the Angels. He had received the healing that he needed and was looking forward to going to the light, said his goodbyes and was off within minutes. Starr was so relieved and pleased that this finally took place. It had been many years that her Dad had been around, and she could not express in words the gratitude she felt.

There are countless more stories. The Angels wanted you to know that there are no limitations, not even in heaven. And that everything happens just the way it should; the healing will occur when it is the right time. Be open to the healing Spirits want to give, if it"s for you or maybe for a deceased loved one.

Chapter Twenty-Two
Crossing Over

There are really no words to describe the pain of what it is like when a loved one crosses over to the other side, to the spirit world. If you are experiencing this right now, I send you healing energy to sustain you and keep pulling you through.

Our deceased loved ones want us to move on with our life. They do not measure how much you cry for them, or how that equates to how much you loved them. They know that you have a life to live and do not want to hold you back. In fact, many of them do not want to go to the light until they are sure that you will be all right. Why would we want to deprive them of that satisfaction? Why would we want to rob them of that pleasure?

When we die, the physical body ceases to function; rather, it passes from one form of existence (physical) to a higher, exclusively spiritual form of existence. God created us all with a yearning for Eternity. We never really die; we just change in forms and worlds.

Your spirit, your soul, the essence of you will live forever.

As a natural-born Medium, I have seen dead people all of my life. However, it is especially personal when a loved one comes through from beyond to give you messages.

I remember my father's passing and how difficult that was. He had Alzheimer's, and that disease can take a very long time to progress; but I believe we go when we are ready, and not a minute sooner.

My Dad was having difficulty swallowing his food. In fact, he would forget to swallow his food, and this was brutal to watch. It is so painful seeing someone else suffering, especially a loved one.

Toward the end of his life, Dad was crying and telling everyone he was sorry. I told him I loved him and forgave him for everything. It is a great idea to do this, because that way the person can die in peace.

Sometimes you might notice that the spirit has left the body, although the person is still breathing, this is what happened with my Dad. I could actually see his spirit leave his body. I was standing next to him and my husband Carey was by my side. I could see a white light leave his body. The light was coming out from the top of his head and going toward the heavens. Carey decided he wanted to ask Dad if there was anything he wanted to say before he left. My Dad said, "Yes, tell my wife I love her very much and say hello to Anna Maria and Gertrude." We asked Mom what that meant; but she said she had no idea who those people were. Carey and I looked at each other with puzzlement.

My Mom had an incredibly hard time with Dad's passing. She could no longer live in the house where they had spent almost fifty-five years together. I offered that Mom could stay with us for a while, and she gladly accepted. For about three months, she stayed with us and one of my sisters, Mary, in Miami. I was determined to find her a place where she would be able to cope better. I always knew she would be living in the retirement home next to our house. Even when my Dad was alive, I would tell my Mom, "Mom, one day you will be living in these condos," and she would laugh and say, "That would be nice. I like those condos."

Well, as fate would have it, her desire was coming true. I started looking at some of the nearby condos and found one at a good price, with a view she liked. But all of a sudden, just before I sent the fax to put in the offer, I heard a loud voice, just like a real live person saying, "Look in the computer now. Your Mom's house is in there." I thought I was hearing things or making it up in my mind. I was selling real estate at the time, so this was easy enough to do.

Well, what do you know? A new listing was on the market. I asked Mom, "Do you want to go look at this other property before we make this offer?" She said, "Sure, why not?" We made the appointment and walked into the condo. My Mom could not take the smile off her face.   The apartment had fabulous energy, and everywhere you turned, there was an angel - either on the living room wall, on the dresser, in the kitchen, you name it. The house was full of angels. We walked into the guest room and there was a picture on the wall, exactly like the one my Mom and Dad used to have in their living room. We took this as a sign.

My Mom was so thrilled, she kept pushing me, saying, "Hurry, go put an offer on this house. I do not want to lose it!" I happily went back home to write up the offer, looked up the tax roll of the property, printed it out and started to type up the contract. All of a sudden, I saw the name Gertrude and immediately got goose bumps all over my body. I felt my Dad's energy, and I heard him say, "I gave you the message." My Dad had known this property would be on the market three months before he passed. He was letting me know the name so that I would not have any doubt about the blessing that would be bestowed. He wanted this property for my Mom, and knew she deserved it. That condo is like a model home; absolutely beautiful, just like her. We also found and met Anna Maria shortly after his passing.

We are always getting messages. We just have to listen. The next story I am about to tell you is about my brother Mario. As you know, he was battling cancer and did not make it, but this story will give you a clear indication of how powerful the spirit world is.

My brother Mario was a very shy guy, pretty much a loner. He kept to himself, and would never hurt a fly. I would have to say he was definitely a workaholic. He never really took good care of himself, but was always so kind to others. Mario had been suffering from back pain for almost ten years.

He would take medication, hoping the pain would go away. He never got himself checked out medically and would say he did not have time for that because he had to attend to his clients. He owned his own electronic company and would fix registers. He never put himself first or gave himself much importance.

He was the kindest man you could ever meet, with a heart so pure and loving; a heart full of gold. He always told me he thought I was different and said he knew there was more there than meets the eye. He said he liked to listen to the coast-to-coast radio station at midnight because the program talked about metaphysical subjects. He said I should talk on this radio station so that listeners could benefit from what I had to say.

I remember when Mario first told me he had cancer. He did not want to believe it and said, "Elsa, I do not want to die." I told him, "I know you are not going to die." I did not want to accept his imminent death, either. Before his passing, we all gathered around his bed, held hands and started to pray. I said, "Mario, we all love you so much. You have no idea how much you are loved."

He was in a coma-like state. However, one tear came out of his right eye, so we knew he could hear us. We started praying and the Holy Spirit just took over me. It was beautiful. I started singing Mario a song I had never heard before. It was a time of peace and love, such sadness, but with serenity at the core.

When I kissed him on the forehead to say good-bye, I knew it would be the last time I would see him in physical form. The day before, spirits had already shown me everything that would happen, like watching a movie. I had the most astonishing gift of actually seeing his spirit leave his body. We were driving on the turnpike. I was in the passenger seat and I saw his spirit leave his body. It was a bright white light that left his heart. Then he was looking back at his life, showing me his memories. He said, "Look" and I did. He showed me his childhood, things that took place and things he regretted. He said, "Bye, Elsa," and I said "Bye, Mario." Then I saw Angels take his spirit up to the heavens. I knew that my Grandma was there to greet him; she had already "told" me that morning that she was waiting for him, and would take good care of him. Two seconds later, my sister Irene called. She had been staying with Mario in the hospital and started out, "Elsa," but before she could continue, I said, "I know, he showed me the whole thing." My brother was no longer scared of death; he was enjoying an indescribable peace. What an awesome gift! How could I ask for anything more?

With this experience, I would have to say I have had a taste of what it is like to die. Even though it was my brother's experience, he was letting me in on this gift.

In the next chapter, you will read how I had a near death experience, what I saw and the messages that I received.

"We must not Wait"

We must not wait to show our love to those our hearts hold dear. For within our hearts we know that God is the one who brought them here.

So why don't we express our love and gratitude the way our loved ones want to hear? For tomorrow might be too late to express the joy, and the tears.

What would it take to touch a soul, to reach the essence that makes them whole? To make a difference in their life, to give them the courage to try. To be the one to catch their fall, to lift them up so they stand tall.

For all tomorrows start today, our life is borrowed, and then taken away. So express your love today!

Elsa J. Stokes Copyright © 2009

Chapter Twenty-Three
When the Angels Took My Hand

Growing up with the gift of prophecy has its advantages; always knowing what would happen next felt very safe for me, regardless of the situation. I felt like I was being warned ahead of time when I would receive these visions. I was given these visions, I believed, so that I would be able to handle anything that came my way. I felt obliged to God and was something I never took for granted.

Well, the next story I am about to tell left me in a state of shock. Although I was given signs as to what would happen along the way, nothing could prepare me for the experience of what felt like my own death.

In the previous chapter I had told God the name of the guy I wanted to meet and what I wanted him to look like. God showed me where I would find him and that I would be his girl by the end of the night. The guy turned out to be an angel sent from God.

It was 1992. I was living with my parents, studying, working and getting my life together. I was also very passionate about working out.

I started dating this gentleman, let's call him John. He was a very funny guy, liked to make people laugh, was very outgoing and really knew how to have a good time. He

had a roommate at the time. We'll call him Bob. The two guys were very close and did almost everything together. One day while we were all having dinner at their house, Bob told John that his Mom had to have an operation. She was having problems with her ovaries. I told John that I had an overwhelming feeling I should go visit Bob's Mom before she was operated on. John said, "You do not even know her." He thought it was a strange request. I told him, "Please do not question me; this is something that I have to do." He said, "OK, I will tell Bob to call his Mom and let her know you are going to go visit her."

The next day rolled around and I was very determined to go visit Bob's Mom, let's call her Lynn, to comfort her and let her know she would be all right.

My best friend tried to stop me from going. "You are so crazy, Elsa. You do not even know her. She is going to think you are so strange." I told her I did not care, that nothing would stop me from going to see Lynn that night. My friend wanted to come along, but I told her it was best I go alone. I wanted to reflect on what I was going to tell Lynn, and felt that our connection was going to be very special.

I arrived at the hospital and passed right by her room. Then a gentleman called out, "Elsa, is that you?" I said yes, and he said, "Come on in." I did and everyone there was praying the rosary. I felt like I was home because I grew up in the Catholic faith. I handed Lynn a card and told her, "I wrote this poem just for you. God wants you to know that you are going to be all right, and that all the Angels in heaven are watching over you."

She looked a little concerned about what would happen next. Then her husband told me, "It is a great thing that you came to see a total stranger, and drove such a long distance to do it. God is going to bless you. Maybe you will hear from us and we will nominate you to come to this special spiritual retreat we are having. It would be quite an honor to be chosen." I smiled and said, "Oh that would be great."
I left there happy, with the anticipation of receiving a call from them soon.

I was always very spiritual. I would attend Sunday mass, and almost every Thursday night I would go to prayer meeting. God was a very important part of my life. I was attending a Charismatic Catholic Church at the time. I thought it was so fascinating how the Holy Spirit would take over my body and I would start speaking in tongues. I also found it astonishing how everyone would get slain by the Spirit. This is when the Deacon puts his hand over your head and you pass out; you fall back into the arms of someone behind you.

One day at prayer meeting, I got the courage to try. I always wondered what it would feel like, and wanted to experience it firsthand. As I started to go up to the altar, I could hear the voices of Angels. It was so beautiful. I could not understand what they were saying, but I could hear whispers in my ears. I walked up, looked at the Deacon, smiled and instantly passed out.

I had been lying on the floor for the entire thirty-minute service. Finally someone woke me up and said, "Get up, the service is over." I guess no one is supposed to bother you while you are being blessed by the presence of God. The Deacon told me he had never seen anyone pass out for so long before; the norm was only a few minutes. He asked me if I could tell him what I experienced. I told him I was so glad no one had woken me up. I do not remember what happened, only that there was total silence and stillness, and I knew something very special had just taken place.

When I started driving home from the service, I asked God if there was any way he would give me the gift to put my hands on someone and assist them to get slain by the spirit. Then I heard a voice that said, "It is already done."

The next morning I wanted to try the procedure on my best friend, since I had received the clearance from God. I was so excited, and I asked my friend, "Will you let me put my hand over you?" She said yes. I told her God wants to bless you, and she trusted me and let me do it. I made sure there was someone behind her to catch her. I put my hand over her head and it worked! It was so easy. I did not have to do anything. The Holy Spirit just took over. I was so amazed; I started asking every one of my friends. All of a sudden I was being called to peoples" homes I did not know to help those who were going through rough times. I was in my glory and felt honored that God was using me to help.

I made it a common practice to read the Bible every day and asked God what He wanted to tell me for that day. I would just pray over the Bible, open it exactly where the perfect message was waiting for me, and receive the message that was specific to that day.

I received such promising messages, messages of hope, surrender and love. On this particular day, I opened up the Book of Job in the Bible. It describes how Job, a good man, loses everything and suffers total disaster. He gets sick and is put to the test to see how much faith he has in God. He never gives up on God, and God eventually gives him twice as much as he had before.

When I was reading this section, I did not want to believe that something terrible would happen to me, so I tried to brush it off and just went on with my day.

Nighttime had arrived. I used to love to work out until the gym closed, after midnight. I got home just past midnight and was getting ready to go to sleep, when I heard a voice say, "Open the Bible again and get your message for today." I could not believe it when the page opened to the section on Job. I was taken aback. What did God want to tell me?

I said a prayer and went to bed, then started to pray my rosary. Ten minutes into the rosary, I felt an excruciating pain in my lower stomach and started screaming at the top of my lungs. My Mom and Dad ran into the room and asked what was wrong? "I do not know," I said, "but I am in so much pain, I cannot take it." They quickly got dressed and said, "Come on, we are going to the hospital, this is not normal." I got dressed and dragged myself into the car but could not stop crying. My Dad was so nervous he could not find the hospital. It also did not help that there was a lot of construction work at the time and all the roads looked the same.

I did not want to upset him further, so I told him to take me home. I said, "You know what, it must just be a cramp I got from working out. Take me to the 24- hour drug store, I will get some Icy Hot, and everything will be okay." He looked at me and said, "Are you sure? I said, "Yes, the pain will go away." I did not want to accept that anything bad was happening to me.

We came back home, I rubbed some Icy Hot on my stomach, and went back to bed. I slept for only about half an hour but the pain returned. I started screaming once again at the top of my lungs. This time my Dad was prepared. He took me to a different hospital in Miami that he was sure he would find.

It was just past three o'clock in the morning and the service at this hospital was poor, to say the least. They did the standard blood test, along with an ultrasound and every other test known to man. But they could not find anything wrong with me. In the meantime, my stomach started blowing up like a balloon. I could not even go to the bathroom. The lady who shared the room with me kept screaming, "This girl is going to die, help her. Can't you see her stomach?" This was not helping my pain.

The doctors did not know what to do and decided to cut me open to see what was going on. I agreed, since I could not take the pain any more. I asked to see the doctor who was going to operate on me before I agreed to sign the papers.

Well, in comes a totally drunk doctor, screaming out my name, "Elsa. Who is Elsa? Where is Elsa?" He came close to me and all I could smell was the hard whisky he had been drinking just minutes before.

I was not about to trust my life to this drunk man. At that point, he was not a doctor to me; he was just a drunk. I got a clear sign to get out of that hospital! My sister Angela was very concerned as well as the rest of the family. Please let this man operate on you, everyone would say, or else you are going to die, please do it for us.

I called on my Angels to help: Angels, please tell me what to do. Just at that second I thought of John, and wished he could be there. Well, not two minutes later, he beeped me. I asked the nurse to let me borrow her phone. It was about five o'clock in the morning and I thought John would be sleeping. I called him back, and the first thing he said was, "What is wrong? Something woke me up and told me to reach you. I know something is wrong." I started crying, because I knew the angels had sent him. I told John what was going on and he said he would come over right away and take me to another hospital. I could tell he was very nervous; after all, my life was on the line.

The hospital had me sign papers saying that they were not responsible if I died. The doctor told me, "We have taken a lot of blood from you, lady, and we are recommending that you get this operation done here and now." I gladly signed the papers and totally trusted in the Angels and the messages I was getting to go to the other hospital.

John came in like a speeding bullet; he was on a mission. My parents followed him to the other hospital, and it turned out that he took me back to the hospital that my Dad could not find in the first place. We arrived there and everyone was very nice. I could see the concerned look on the nurses' faces. I told them what had happened and they said they would have to do the exact same exams and tests as in the previous hospital. I told them I understood.

After the entire tests were done, the doctor recommended I take some antibiotics and said that he would check on me in the morning. I was so weak, I really did not have much energy to think, plus I was given heavy medication for the pain.

My Dad was not feeling comfortable with the idea. He had been asking Mother Mary to come and help. He was getting a clear message to step in and get a second opinion, to call the family doctor to come in and see me. The doctor did not have a problem with that.

My Dad attempted to call our family doctor, but he

did not answer, so he left an urgent message with the receptionist: "Doctor, you know my beautiful daughter, Elsa. She is in danger and I really need your help." The doctor rushed right over to the hospital to see me. He was always so nice and would come to our house to treat everyone in the family. I always thought everyone had a doctor who made house calls. But he only did this for us first, because there were so many of us, and second, because he really took a liking to our family.

The family doctor looked at me and said," You must operate on her immediately. If you do not, she will not live. She will not last until the morning, like you are suggesting, Doctor."

The doctor agreed and I was prepped for an operation. They gave me about fifteen minutes to visit with everyone before I went in to the operating room.

My Mom was the last one to visit me. She looked into my eyes and said, "I am so sorry you are going through this. Be strong. Remember that lady Lynn? You did not know her but you drove more than an hour to see her and told her she was going to be all right. God was preparing you to be strong for this; the doctors are telling you now that they might have to remove both of your ovaries. God has a plan; we just have to trust. I believe in God, and remember, any time anything bad happens, something good will follow or there is something good in the bad; you just have to find it." I held her hand and said, "Mom, you have always been such an

Angel in my life." She smiled and could not take her eyes off of me.

It was time. I took a deep breath and told God, "If you want to take me, I am not scared. Thy will be done."

The nurses rolled me over to the operating bed and started pushing the bed toward the operating room; I looked at everyone for what I thought might be the last time and said my goodbyes in my mind, just in case I did not make it back.

I entered the operating room. The doctor was friendly enough. He said, "Just breathe into this mask and in a few seconds you will be out, you will not remember anything." I said, "OK" and started breathing into the mask. In what felt like minutes, I had come out of my body. I was a spirit out of my body. I could see Angels in the room and other Spirits. Some Spirits had an image of a face and a body and others just had a shape or color. Some of these shapes and colors I had never seen before.

I noticed that I could hear what everyone was saying, so I yelled out, "I can hear you" to the doctor. I saw myself completely opened up, on the operating table. It was so surreal. I did not even know this person on the operating table; she had no spirit and no soul.

I decided I wanted to look around, since I realized that I could see everything that was going on. I wanted to see what my family was doing. Maybe they would see me. I saw my Mom leaning on my Dad's shoulder; she looked so worried. I saw my sister Angela holding my Mom's hand. Angela was very sad. I saw John walking around, trying to take a peek into the operating room. His expression looked very concerned. Then I saw one of my girlfriends trying to flirt with John; great friend she turned out to be!

I tried to touch my Mom's hand, but she did not feel anything. I looked like a ghost, the ghost I had been seeing all my life. I thought for sure I was dead.

Then I heard a beautiful song coming from the operating room. I went back there to see how I was doing. Apparently I had lost a lot of blood and they had to call out for more blood. So they had my body in limbo for a while. Suddenly, I felt a rush come over me, and I started to travel up. My spirit was moving up. I could see gold light with a circle of white light around it. The light started to get brighter and brighter, then turned into a translucent white color. A feeling of indescribable love I have never experienced before came over me, and the song the Angels were singing became louder and louder.

Then, all of the sudden, I saw an Angel in front of me to my left. She grabbed my hand and said, 'Do you want to come?" Before I could answer, I saw another Angel on my right. He said to me, "You are safe. Would you like to come with us?" I looked down at my body below me and said, "No, I do not want to go. I want to have a baby and I cannot do this to my family." I saw how devastated they were and I just could not go.

They said, "Please remember, you can have anything you want, anyone can. All you have to do is believe." They instantaneously let go of my hand. It felt like I flew right back into my body. It happened so fast that I do not think I could explain its speed or it could even be measured.

The next thing I remember was waking up and the nurse showing me a picture of myself cut open, with a huge mass in my ovary. She said, "Wow, we did not think you were going to make it. You lost a lot of blood but you were so strong, no one could understand it. The doctor is documenting this as a mystery file. Your left ovary had twisted, caused a huge blood clot, and created a big mass. He has removed the left ovary. The good news is that it was not cancerous. The doctor said you were only three hours from death. If you had not gotten this operation, you would be dead." Little did the doctor know that I had just experienced the closest thing to being dead than anyone could ever imagine.

Here is a poem I wrote when this happened in my life.

"As I Lay"

As I lay still on this cold, flat hospital bed, thoughts of uncertainty roll through my head. Oh God, help me through this day.

Another hour, another minute, it's all the same when hurt is running through your veins.

What could I have done differently not to end up this way? Tears run down my face as I try to control the pain.

The doctor warns me that I might not bear a child; things might get complicated for a while. I'm trying to control myself, as I want so much to scream out loud.

Lord, explain it to me somehow.

The very thing I wanted out of life is about to disappear in front of my eyes. As I hear a newborn baby cry, I ask myself, Lord, why?

But still I hold a sparkle of hope in my eyes; Lord, let it be Your will and not mine.

God, I know you have a plan, just help me to try to understand. Ask and you shall receive, no matter how far the dream may seem.

As my Mom looks into my eyes, she sees the sadness that words could never describe.

She tries to comfort me with her touch. Oh God, there is nothing like a Mom's love.

At this point I just want to live to see the sunset again. To be able to hold on to love, to appreciate all that God can give.

A smile, a touch, a warm embrace, it all comes from God's loving grace.

Lord, my eyes were blind from the love you gave.

I was too busy trying to run my own race.

Peace and tranquility run through my mind as I realize my life is not mine.

Oh, how wonderful life can be, if only people took the time to see. Lord, if I had a choice again, I'd do it all so differently.

So, as I lay my head to rest, the doctor whispered in my ear," The *results came out negative." Tears of happiness cannot explain. Oh God, thank you for this day!*

Spirits are so amazing. When I was about eighteen years old, I remember going to the beach one day and seeing a girl in a bikini. She had a big line across her bikini line, from a C-section. I looked at her and said that is going to be me one day.

Another thing I noticed was that for two years before this incident happened to me, I would have nightmares of this exact pain. It would wake me up from my dreams in a sweat, with this excruciating pain. I believe God was preparing me for when it happened to me in real life. I am convinced that if I had never experienced that pain before, I would have had no other choice than to kill myself. It was that painful.

The Angels made it very clear. They said, "You can have anything you u want. All you have to do is believe it." I believe we do not cross over until we are ready to go. I also believe we will come back again and again until we learn all of our lessons and become more and more like God.

We really do not have any limitations, only the ones

we create. Go out and create your world just the way you desire. It belongs to you. You are so precious in the eyes of God. Go to your Angels often; you will be fascinated as to what they can do.

I must tell you that the Angels wanted me to end this message with their song. I remembered this was the song that I sang when my brother was passing, and the one that I heard when I had my near-death experience.

"I hear you calling me"

I hear you calling me. I hear your voices in my ear. I hear you calling me, loud and clear, love, love divine. I hear you whisper in my ear, love, love divine. I am here, I am home, I hear you calling me. I see your hands reach out for me. I hear you calling me. Let me know where I will be, love, love divine, show me to the light, love, love divine, show me to the light.

Even though the angels are the ones singing the song, it is as if though we are singing it to them.

9 7 8 0 6 1 5 4 9 7 2 1 1